.

# THE JEWEL IN THE WOUND

# THE
# JEWEL
## IN THE
# WOUND

*How the body expresses*
*the needs of the psyche and*
*offers a path to transformation*

❋

ROSE-EMILY ROTHENBERG

Chiron Publications
Wilmette, Illinois

*Editing / Jane LeCompte*

*Book and cover design / Susan Kress Hamilton*
*Phineas, Portsmouth, New Hampshire*

*Printing / Penmor Lithographers, Lewiston, Maine*

Art on the cover is from
*Codex Palatinus Latinus 1066*, folio 230v, by Johannes Ridevallus (f. 1330),
"Fulgentius Metaforallus." © Biblioteca Apostolica Vaticana.
Reprinted with permission from the Vatican Library.

Library of Congress Cataloging-in-Publication Data

Rothenberg, Rose-Emily, 1939-
    The jewel in the wound : how the body expresses the needs of the
psyche and offers a path to transformation / Rose-Emily Rothenberg.
        p. cm.
    Includes bibliographical references and index.
    ISBN 1-888602-16-3 (alk. paper)
    1. Psychoanalysis. 2. Jungian psychology. 3. Mind and body. 4.
Rothenberg, Rose-Emily, 1939-    . I. Title.
    BF173 .R66 2001
    150.19'54--dc21

                                                    2001003984

For my mother
because she didn't get to know me

"...what the jewel signifies:
it is a *God-redeemer*, a renewal of the sun....
The renewed God signifies a regenerated attitude,
a renewed possibility of life,
a recovery of vitality...."


C.G. Jung
*Psychological Types*, CW 6
Princeton, NJ: Princeton University Press, 1971
pars. 297, 301

# TABLE OF CONTENTS

# LIST OF ILLUSTRATIONS

# PREFACE

Each of us is given a task to perform in this lifetime — to carry and transform our individual piece of the universe. The loss of my mother shortly after my birth created the wound that made it possible for me to accomplish my task.

I was guided in this process by dreams and visions that offered entry to the collective unconscious[1], the deepest layer of the unconscious and the realm that lies beyond the personal mother. Working with these gifts from the unconscious as well as with painting and clay, I kept the flame that had never been completely extinguished between my mother and me. Even more important, this work let me create and then strengthen an ongoing conscious connection to a deeper layer of the psyche. This connection made up for what my mother could not do and simultaneously provided a path to find her.

During times of transition in my journey, spontaneous scars arose on my body. Born from the psychic wounds and challenges of these passages, the scars — which I at first abhorred — ultimately rescued me. Because they mirrored my psychological condition in the outer world, they enticed me to investigate their meaning. Throughout my life the scars have continued to inspire me, bringing to birth the unborn parts of my psyche.

My spirit for life did not die with my mother; rather, it took up residence within the scars. After years of investigation, I now see that they were the objects upon which I projected[2] the suffering from the chaos in my early life; yet they also held the numinosity of the jewel I longed to discover. They were tangible and real, but they also offered me an experience of the eternal that linked the spirit and the body, life and death, my mother and me.

My curiosity about the evolution of the scars initially took me into analysis. There I worked on my psyche, the ground from which the scars sprang. It would take many life experiences, including marriage, motherhood, and illness, to concentrate my inner work enough to promote healing and wholeness. The suffering and the work created a path I could take to find my mother, illustrating that renewal is at hand even in the lowest of conditions. My mother, returning to me in a dream, satisfied a lifelong yearning so intense that I don't think I would have had the resolve to go on with my life and my work without this reunion.

To maintain a living connection with my mother, I kept up an active relationship to the unconscious. The creative energy flowing from that relationship ultimately carried me to Africa, where scars are purposely created by indigenous people in the ritual art of scarification. I interviewed shamans and gained a deeper understanding of the spiritual nature that I knew was alive in my own scars. Thus I was able to reconnect to the collective layer of the psyche that exists before the mother: what the alchemists called the *prima materia*, the psychic ingredients (literally, "first matter") that influence how our lives will unfold.

I needed many nurturing experiences from inside and outside to help me integrate and transform my relationship to the dark realities of life. What I came to appreciate was that what comes up from the body and the unconscious begins in dark form. Psychologically, these dark realities mark the birth of something striving to come forth from the unconscious into consciousness; symbolically, they represent the jewel that has been lost and that carries the new potential.

The cover of this book illustrates this archetypal event. The picture is from an alchemical version of Botticelli's painting "The Birth of Venus." In this picture "Venus stands on her scallop shell, her body all roses: the red flowering out of the white."[3] The growth of the pearl out of the shell is the basis of this symbolic representation.[4] Venus is born out of the chaos of the world's beginnings, out of the Self's coming to birth — a dark beginning that is often forgotten and denied when beauty stands so present. But black is the beginning of the alchemical opus (the individual alchemist's lifework, or in Jungian nomenclature, individuation). The whitening is the sorting, the transformation and the integration of the *prima materia*, finally leading out of the darkness into the red of feelings. This is the life-giving principle that incubates in the dark and breaks through.

As I began to reshape more of myself and my life, the physical scars themselves began to take on a different shape. My evolving consciousness and repeated experiences of renewal out of chaos continued to be reflected in my body. Psychologically, I was able to travel more easily in the inner world and then, literally, in the outer world, as is reflected in the pages that follow.

In this book I expose to the light of day a very personal and private account of individuation. A journey of this sort is sacred and thus deserves care and protection lest damage be done to the soul. At first this prompted me to ask the question: by making this inner journey public, will I violate the soul? I had to weigh this against the meaning my personal journey could bring to people who have had similar experiences and are searching for answers. Then I remembered a dream I had many years ago which helped me settle the question. In the dream, the building where I went for treatments for my scars had turned into "Bollingen Press" (a reference to the Bollingen Foundation that made possible the publication in English of Jung's *Collected Works*).

Each person who goes deeply into suffering can bring a revelation into living reality. For me the primary mode of revelation was spontaneously arising scars, a "spontaneous scarification." These scars are permanent reminders of the wounds that result from the struggle and challenge to have a conscious, living relationship with God, and of the divine rewards of this relationship. Each one of us is made in the image of God; thus, our suffering is a reflection of God's suffering. As we carry this suffering of God in its multitude of manifest forms, we make a contribution to the collective unconscious as well as to the collective consciousness of our time.

Telling this story of suffering the wound and finding the jewel it conceals has been an enterprise whose healing spirit has become a conscious reality for me. I have written this book to give back what I was given in the opportunity to participate in this divine drama. This gift has also enabled me as a Jungian analyst to help others, through analytic work, find the jewel in their own unique wounds, the jewel that awaits rescue. My own work continues.

July 2001                                               Rose-Emily Rothenberg

# ACKNOWLEDGMENTS

Many people accompanied me and supported this book since its inception. My manuscript had the benefit of excellent editorial assistance from Judy Ross, who read many early drafts of my writing until it was shaped into a book. Early versions were edited by Priscilla Stuckey and Kate Smith Hanssen. Many helpful comments came from reviews by George Elder, Janet Dallett, Louise Mahdi and Susan Rublaitus. Lore Zeller and Nancy Mozur of the C.G. Jung Institute of Los Angeles library and bookstore offered research and gracious support. Betty Meador, Dennis Slattery, Donald Sandner, Meredith Sabini and Suzanne Wagner gave important guidance along the way. Deborah Wesley and Michael Gellert helped me craft the manuscript with great feeling and psychological acumen. Of course, I take full responsibility for the final product, which is mine alone.

I owe special thanks to Susan Dworski for her expert suggestions in preparing the manuscript. My gratitude also goes to Burkina Faso filmmaker Edouard Yé for capturing with his photographic skill most of the pictures of the people, scenery and ceremonies in Africa and to Marcel Ouattara, Edouard Yé, and Théophane Thou for making our visit to Burkina Faso both possible and incredibly meaningful. I also want to thank Reed Hutchinson of the UCLA Photographic Services and Susan Einstein for preparing many of the transparencies for the book's illustrations.

My ventures into the inner world of my dreams and visions and accompanying amplifications evolved from discussions with my analysts, mentors and colleagues: Max Zeller, Hilde and James Kirsch, Edward Edinger, Theodore Abt and Hermann Strobel. My forays into the outer world of art, culture and travel to Africa were assisted by Doran Ross, Director of the UCLA Fowler Museum of Cultural History, and Malidoma Somé, an elder and diviner from the Dagara people of West Africa, and a widely-known writer and lecturer. I also feel a deep gratitude to all the people in Africa who resonated with my reason for being there and who openly shared their spirit and wisdom with me.

My gratitude goes to Murray Stein for appreciating the message of the book and bringing about its publication by Chiron. The design and production of this book reflects the expert skill of Susan Kress Hamilton at

Phineas, and the excellent editorial guidance of Jane LeCompte. I also want to thank my son, Joshua, and his wife, Pam, for their nurturing during my work on this project.

Finally, for unequaled love, support and assistance and for his generosity with his time, his patience, and his deep appreciation for my process, I am indebted to my husband, Les, who stood by me throughout the lengthy process of preparing this book.

Every reasonable effort has been made to locate the owners of rights to previously published works reprinted here. We gratefully acknowledge permission to reprint the following:

C.G. Jung, *Collected Works* and *"Nietzche's Zarathustra: Notes of the Seminar Given in 1934–1939."* © Various dates by Princeton University Press. Reprinted by permission of Princeton University Press and Routledge.

Jolande Jacobi (ed.), *Paracelsus: Selected Writings.* © 1951 by Bollingen Foundation; renewed 1979 by Princeton University Press. Reprinted by permission of Princeton University Press.

Joseph Campbell, *The Mythic Image.* © 1981 by Princeton University Press. Reprinted by permission of Princeton University Press.

The author and publisher also wish to thank the custodians of the works of art and photographs (acknowledged in the credit lines for the illustrations) for supplying them and granting permission to use them.

# WORKING WITH A BODY SYMPTOM

*To explore a body symptom is to enter it, as it has entered us,*
*and to partake in a sacred mystery. It is with the greatest respect*
*and humility that we undertake this task.*

This book addresses the individuation process initiated by a body symptom and the multiple benefits gained when one explores the symptom at many levels, as I have done with the keloid scar. Becoming more conscious is one of the main goals of this work, and perhaps this is one of the intentions of the psyche in presenting us with a body symptom. Physical symptoms in their most positive, metaphorical sense are like jewels in the body awaiting discovery. They create the impetus for the patient to do the inner work, and they carry the nucleus for the cure. The body symptom serves a definite purpose in this regard, directing one to the source of the disease or the disorder that created it, and thus to healing.

There are multiple influences that contribute to the evolution, meaning, and healing of illness or disease. Genetic structure, environmental conditions, and psychological components are a few of the aspects to be considered. Each disorder is unique to the person who has it. In determining the psychic component of the diagnosis (and there is always psychic content), one needs to look at every aspect of the person's life (i.e., the attitude toward the body and its manifestations, the conditions at the moment of illness and its recurrence, etc.). It would be difficult to endure the wound if one did not see it in its total aspect — the literal events surrounding the onset, the developmental aspects, and the archetypal underpinnings. Discovering the archetype[5] behind a body symptom can be the turning point in one's journey as the symptom reveals its place in one's personal myth.

Body symptoms usually emerge from the inner depths into the light of day quite unexpectedly. When illness erupts, one abruptly faces the reality that one is not the only ruler of one's own house. One is forced to pay attention to the psyche, because it has become real. When a physical symptom appears, something inside that can't reach consciousness directly manifests in a physiological form. By doing so, it assists the ego by carrying the content that the ego cannot easily absorb.

One symptom can have many levels of meaning. The depth of one's insight into the symptom depends on where the psyche is in its evolution and on the ego's tenacity in undertaking the exploration. By delving into the symptom's depths and following its symbolic nature, one is led to the archetypal layer[6] of the psyche, where transformation and renewal are possible.

Body symptoms are carriers of personal and collective memories, archetypes, and instincts from which we have been disconnected. Great effort is needed to reconnect to these lost and forgotten elements and to perceive the meaning of the disease. Diligent attention to dreams and visions that center around the specific body symptom can be helpful, because they reveal the deeper layers of the symptom's meaning. Gathering personal and archetypal associations furthers the analysis and understanding of the psychological and symbolic components of a physical symptom. The archetypal base of symptoms discloses the collective level of the unconscious, the deepest roots within the psyche. Reaching this level brings a broad dimension and a symbolic meaning to the individual symptom. This larger context gives the ego a place from which to work and to integrate the experience of illness. It gives meaning to the experience of suffering. One significant meaning is having to relate to reality as it is.

Jung wrote: "[T]he self has its roots in the body, indeed in the body's chemical elements."[7] According to Jung, the Self is the name for the whole psyche, the central archetype of the collective unconscious, the unifying center of the psyche. The Self carries the god-image. In illness an aspect of the Self becomes manifest in the body, in matter. Through analytic work, the conscious ego can bring symbolic meaning to bear on this physiological manifestation of the Self. In disease, the Self is making the ego aware of itself. In so doing, it brings to the suffering of illness an intensity and a numinosity, as if the gods were meeting the individual and becoming manifest. Symptoms and images that are persistently numinous tell a story that must be heard. The power of the Self is behind them, and the living spirit is within them.

Disease was originally thought to be caused by spirit possession and loss of soul. Healing, consequently, came through identifying and dispelling the evil spirit(s). With the advancement of biology and science, attention focused on causes and healing processes that reside exclusively in the body. With this, psyche and body experienced a decisive separation that Jung and depth psychology have tried to address. As Jung said, "Probably in absolute reality there is no such thing as body and mind, but body and mind or soul are the same, the same life, subject to the same laws, and what the body does is happening in the mind."[8] In its conceptualization of the psyche and the body, depth psychology encompasses both the spiritual and the material dimension. What is expressed in the body is understood to have a psychological equivalent.

As the psyche incarnates, it is born into flesh. We help to bring the psyche further into the world through contemplation, introspection, questioning, and research in the outer, medical world as well as in the interior world of the soul and the unconscious. As a result of this process, something in the psyche changes, even if the physical symptom doesn't. The ego helps activate healing and attempts to meet the unknown forces halfway. The very nature of reflection and integration brings light and energy, strengthening the ego. The same analytical attitude can be used whether working with body symptoms or with psychological symptoms. One needs to consider the manifestation of the symptom at the literal level (how it functions organically) as well as to identify its psychological and symbolic components.

In analyzing body symptoms, alchemical symbolism is quite helpful. For the medieval alchemist, the alchemical work began with containing the raw material in the alchemist's vessel and then descending into the darkness of this *materia* to find the lost value hidden within it. Metaphorically, one descends into a given illness as if one were an alchemist in search of the spirit embedded in matter. This is a heroic undertaking.

Amplifying the disease process through analysis and engaging in artwork that parallels and mirrors the symptom help unveil the symptom's meaning. Often, a lost or hidden aspect comes to light. Becoming conscious of one's dynamics suggests the possibility of some control, whether a darker or a more positive aspect is discovered. This investigation can then lead to a change in the total personality and can further its development. The analytic work does not necessarily change the physical symptom, but it can bring it a greater depth of meaning, *and the meaning can become a guide.*

Within the disease itself resides the cure. This embraces the alchemical principle that the end product and its initial material are "one" and that the one "has everything it needs." Paracelsus, a sixteenth-century physician and alchemist, also wrote about this concept:

> Even while still in the womb, unborn, man is burdened with the potentialities of every disease, and is subject to them. And because all diseases are inherent in his nature, he could not be born alive and healthy if an inner physician were not hidden in him. . . . Each natural disease bears its own remedy within itself. Man has received from nature both the destroyer of health and the preserver of health . . . . what the first strives to shatter and destroy, the innate physician repairs. . . . There where diseases arise, there also can one find the roots of health. For health must grow from the same root as disease, and whither health goes, thither also disease must go.[9]

Symptoms must be considered seriously because they carry urgent messages from deep inside. The deeper the symptom, the more severe or chronic, the more integral it is to one's personal myth. Disease may be among the major life events that help one discover his or her myth. My personal myth is that of the orphan who begins life in solitude or abandonment and then, like the archetypal hero, undertakes the tasks that will lead to the discovery of her/his real identity. Such an early wound — losing a parent or experiencing abandonment — requires considerable healing. This rite of passage involves the death of the old and the birth of the new, and it inevitably creates a wound. If the wound is very deep, sizable healing is necessary.

The orphan, especially, needs something upon which to project the absent parent. The keloid scars that I developed in my youth became this object for me. They arose spontaneously on my body, marking my physical and psychological injuries, reflecting my unique being. They have been overzealous in their reappearance at times of transition, and I have persistently asked: what was the intention of the psyche in creating them? For many years I thought of the scars as an injustice I had to bear, but through this work I now see that they protected me from all I had to withstand. I owe them a great debt.

I was in analysis for thirty years with four Jungian analysts sequentially. I began analysis when I was in my early twenties, generally with one session a week. I ended my analysis when my last analyst retired, several years before I went to Africa when I was in my mid fifties. Many of the early dreams and artwork included in this book I took to my analysis. The insights and amplifications about them are grounded in what I learned from my analysts' interpretations. In subsequent years, I gained additional amplifications from occasional consultations with a few analyst colleagues, along with my own continuing research mainly, but not entirely, in Jung's *Collected Works* and various books on symbols. I synthesized this material with my newly emerging insights and reflections on those early interpretations, and the results are presented in the following pages.

Amplifying the dream images, ruminating on and writing about them, has brought me to ever-new levels of development. Feelings that I hadn't originally experienced helped to congeal and integrate the deeper meanings of these dreams, active imaginations,[10] and artwork. When I reflected on the books, fairy tales, and myths that have had the deepest impact on me and that I have included in this narrative, additional insights came to me. When I could let my imagination mix into the equation, a greater synthesis occurred. All of this material, from the inside and outside, has brought me to this point and to telling this story.

# CHAPTER ONE

# THE COMING OF THE SCARS

*The decisive question for man is:*
*Is he related to something infinite or not?*[11]

I was six days old when my mother died. My birth was her third cesarean. Soon afterward, she developed an infection and died of septicemia. Eleven days later I came home from the hospital alone to my father and two sisters, who were twelve and one and a half. A nursemaid took care of me for nine months. Then other caretakers came and went. A month before I was two years old, my father remarried.

My first memory takes place a few years later. Our newly configured family stood in front of the hall closet, and our stepmother insisted that my sister and I wear leggings to go outside in the cold. My sister didn't want to wear the leggings and yelled, "I don't have to listen to you. You're not our real mother anyway!" That was the first time I was conscious of that fact, and I was stunned into silence.

This announcement foreshadowed unremitting difficulties. From that moment on I was paralyzed by the fear that if I didn't meet with my stepmother's approval and my father's dictate that I do so, I would be abandoned again. The door to spontaneous expression began to close, but the door to the power of the unconscious remained open. Through that door came the first dream I can remember from my childhood. My whole orphan experience was condensed in this dream.

> *I am standing in the center of my childhood house.*
> *Behind me stands a dead tree with bare branches and no leaves.*
> *From my forearm, black snakes are being born.*

I understand this dream today as follows: in the center of my being was my mother's death, and I felt barren without her. The tree is often a symbol of the eternal spirit that sheds its leaves, dying in order to live. The dead tree in my dream, I later realized, carried my mother's soul, and the snakes represented not only my psyche's reaction to this initial trauma but also, ultimately, a way to go beyond it.

Symbolically, snakes convey powerful energies. These energies can be used as poison or as panacea. Snakes exemplify both the most inferior and the most superior in humankind: destruction or divine wisdom. Snakes symbolize the most primitive level of life as well as rebirth and resurrection. They can also represent the incarnation of the dead and, perhaps, in the dream were a container for my mother's spirit. Moreover, the emerging snakes were linked to the scars that were on the verge of announcing themselves. I would come to understand that link in later years.

Before entering school when I was five, I had the required smallpox vaccination. My stepmother asked the doctor to remove a small mole from my other arm at the same time. The procedures were considered routine until scars began to grow on both my arms. Rather than the flat, skin-colored scars that everyone anticipated, my scars reddened and rose up about a quarter of an inch from the surface of the skin. In medical terms, such scars are called keloids, autonomous overgrowths of scar tissue. Everyone was shocked, but my stepmother's reaction was extreme. Before I had a chance to have my own feelings about what was happening, her reaction filled my porous psyche. She was visibly distressed, and my unsightly scars became the subject of intense focus, and not only in seeking medical advice about reducing or removing the scars. She began to watch my every move so I wouldn't injure myself in a way that would create another scar. She was also adamant that I keep the scars hidden from public view. I began to absorb her shame about the scars, and it added to my already entrenched shame at not having my own mother.

Losing my mother and having to relate to a stepmother was what I was given, and I had to endure it. As if to reinforce this painful truth, the psyche next created a vision to help me accept it. Lying on my mother's bed, the bed taken over by my stepmother, and delirious with a high fever, I saw

> across the street, seated at a card table,
> a gypsy is laying out a deck of cards.

Though my four-year-old psyche could not have comprehended its meaning, this vision conveyed the following: these are the cards you are dealt. You have to accept the fate you are given — of living in this world without your mother and being raised by this stepmother.

Around this time I was given a little book that I cherished. I was enchanted with the story, and it too helped me accept my fate. *Wee Fishie Wun*[12] was a story about a little black fish that turned into a beautiful goldfish. In the book, miniature beads of silver and gold were glued on the fish. They were raised from the page and created a knobby effect you could feel. The black fish was a flat picture on the page, but after venturing out in the world to find himself, Wee Fishie Wun was given tiny glistening gold beads, replacing his black beginnings. I especially loved touching the little beads. Although I wasn't conscious of it at the time, I was identifying with the transformation process they represented and which I longed for. The raised beads, or my attraction to them, may also have prefigured the coming of the scars.

A large piece of darkness had penetrated me, and I had internalized it. As a result I felt totally unacceptable and, far more seriously, responsible for bringing it about. The guilt I felt had its beginnings when I was very young, for an uncle had said outright that it was because of me that my mother died. Even though my father replied, "Don't you ever say that to her again!", this remark instilled a culpability that would profoundly affect me. Convinced that I had caused my mother's death, I thought I was to live out my years in continuous repentance.

When our stepmother brought her suitcases in the front door, she offered the promise of warmth and comfort. In reality, however, her presence enveloped me in continued experiences of abandonment. Whenever she didn't get her way, she threatened to pack her bags and leave. I was so afraid of her leaving and of being blamed once again that I buried my own desires and began to shape myself into hers. I became her favorite, for in me she found the outer reflection of her own inner orphan. My stepmother was ripe for the stepmother role. At bottom, she had a fear of life that magnified my own. She couldn't bear to see her own limitations reflected in others, and especially in me. Instead, she wanted me to be what she had hoped for herself. She poured her energy into me, and it gave me a sense of purpose, albeit not my own.

The atmosphere in our house was heavily laden with tension. Her outbursts came and went, as if she were carrying a multitude of sins and feared our misbehavior might reveal them. Her complexes[13] were activated by ours, and ours were excited by hers. Together we experienced a perilous combination of the dark forces that were thrust upon us. I was spellbound under her watchful eye, and my psyche tried to integrate her eye's portentous message. This same tension had appeared in the doctor's office the day of my vaccination; my stepmother suggested the mole be removed out of concern for others' approval.

While my family's focus was on our stepmother, her focus was on the imperfections of those around her. We had to fit into her version of the collective norm and avoid everything that might rouse the imagined disapproval of her friends. Standing before company in a party dress with a loosely tied bow at the back, if I said something she disapproved of, I would feel a yank at the bow.

The psychological makeup of my stepmother mirrored my own psychology, and with this the archetype of the "orphan"[14] came into full bloom. At one point she organized a rummage sale for our local temple. She kept back some of the clothes discarded by the adults she admired and encouraged me and my older sister to wear them. The message was clear: I was to be like the women from whom my stepmother sought approval. However, these "gifts" of clothing came with a price tag: I was beholden to my stepmother.

Her presence intensified my feelings of being of little value. She constantly compared me to my two sisters. When I did something she considered foolish, I was like my oldest sister who didn't openly assert herself. When I did something smart, I was like my other sister who was extraverted, witty and bright. My stepmother was more inhibited by this sister's aggressiveness than able to dominate it, and I looked up to this sister because of this.

Taking the lead from my stepmother, I projected the light and dark sides of myself onto my sisters. I lived under the shadows cast by both of them, but my image of myself fell more in line with the less extraverted one. I was jealous of my more admired sister, but I was emotionally attached to the oldest one. The negative attention this sister elicited was attention nevertheless, and I adopted many of her traits. When my stepmother criticized this sister, I was relieved that she was focusing her rage and frustration on someone else. My subservient position became habitual, and it continued into future relationships. I suppressed my creative individuality in deference to my stepmother's demand for power and dominance.

My oldest sister couldn't survive in the house with the torment she was experiencing. She left several years after our stepmother came and, with my father's help, went to live with an aunt. That left me to be the recipient of our stepmother's aggression. My other sister, one and a half years older than I, survived quite well because of her extraversion. She openly expressed herself, and she refused to do what didn't feel right to her. My father was quite enamored of her. I was too. She was said to "take after" our real mother, and this further elevated her in my eyes. But it was also a source of tremendous pain for me. I wanted to be my father's favorite.

A fantasy play that I engaged in with this sister when I was about eight or nine brought my particular version of the orphan complex to life. One game revealed our identification with opposite sides of the orphan dynamic. Before we went to sleep at night we played out a ritualized drama in our darkened room. I would walk out of the room, turn around, and knock on the door. My sister would come to the door, open it, and find me in an impoverished state. She would take pity on me, invite me in, and ask me who I was and where I was from. I would tell her that I was a widow and that my husband had died in the war. I was left homeless and downtrodden. She would have me sit down at an imaginary table and would provide me with a lavish meal. I had never seen such delicacies as were laid before me. I was finally in the hands of a benevolent and dignified lady who was bestowing nourishment and kindness upon me, and for this I was expected to express unending gratitude. During daytime hours the debt came due. I was in my sister's power. When she made up stories for us to play I had to portray whatever character she chose and to follow the drama as she unfolded it.

My sister became the mother to whom I could belong. She clung to her "ideas of grandeur" to fill the void left by our mother's death. The suffering aspect of the lost orphan fell to me. I lived out the inferior side of the orphan opposites, and the positive side (autonomy and independence) was relegated to the unconscious. I felt I had no right to be alive. The impression I had (though not at a conscious level) was that I wasn't supposed to be here, my mother was. That meant I was living in her place. I felt I could never live up to my image of her, nor could I be a fitting replacement.

My relationship with my father was the one place where I felt received and accepted by virtue of our mutual suffering. I felt he was helpless against the dominant force of my stepmother, and when she said unkind things to him, my reaction was to protect his sensitive feelings as a way of defending against my own. Even as a young child

I tried to shield him from the dark forces neither of us could control — from my stepmother's wrath on the outside and from his depression and mourning on the inside. We were both transfixed by the darkness surrounding us. Although he could not make a substantial change in our situation, he was sympathetic to my plight. He would sometimes bring home presents for my sister and me. He would surprise us with games and puzzles that caught his fancy, and his warmth came wrapped around those little gifts. His sense of humor managed to come out in ways that were very touching.

My father owned and managed a small finance company and would sometimes take me with him to collect money from his customers. I sensed intrigue in these outings to rural areas where the cabins were hidden among the trees, and I loved the time spent alone with him. Yet my father was as introverted as I was, and we would drive along the deserted roads mostly in silence. In those moments it felt as if we were forming a stronger bond. When I was old enough to drive he would let me take the wheel, and that brought me a sense of future independence which was very meaningful to me. He also took me to his office to help him with his work. The books never balanced after I had stood at the counter to accept the payments, but he didn't seem to mind and was very patient with me. I think he knew I needed to get away from the house no matter what the inconvenience or cost. It was his way of offering me an escape, and that was the important thing. These occasions when we were alone together were the happiest of times for me. When we would go out to lunch and walk down the street holding hands I felt like his queen. These precious moments were time stolen away from the painful situation he knew he had, in part, created but was helpless to undo. All along he was supporting my tentative efforts to become an individual, and I wanted to please him more than anything. I wanted him to be proud of me.

My mother's death was not talked about enough for me to absorb its painful truth. I knew it was a tragedy of great proportion to our family and her friends. The only time my father actively acknowledged her death was when my sister and I were confirmed in our local Jewish temple. Afterwards we went to the cemetery with him to put flowers on her grave.

I gathered only a few morsels of my mother's actual life story from relatives, but my imagination embellished these morsels with a multitude of images of what life would have been like if she were still with us. I imagined we would have many visitors and talk for hours about cultural things. The atmosphere would be happy and intellectually nourishing. All this seemed to be hidden away on the third floor of our house where the old suitcases were stored. That floor held the mysteries of her life before I arrived. The luggage held the history of our family when my grandparents were alive. They had taken many journeys to foreign countries and witnessed many things that I could only entertain in my fantasies. I wanted to go where those trunks had traveled, and I adorned these places with my imagination. I would have sat with those suitcases for hours in reverie, but the door to the attic was usually locked, and our stepmother held the key.

Another room on the third floor was more accessible. In this room, the live-in housekeepers stayed. Visiting with them was my refuge, and whenever I could, which was not often enough, I spent time talking with them. I loved to just sit and listen to the stories about their outings with their friends. Their world was far more adventurous and expansive than the one my family inhabited. I also felt their underlying yearnings for a better life, and those yearnings intrigued and comforted me. The only housekeeper who stayed for any length of time was a woman named Maggie. I don't remember when she came, but I remember when she left. Just before my eighth birthday she announced she was leaving to get married. My heart sank, and I suffered a great fear at being in the house without her and having no one to stand between my stepmother and me. Throughout my childhood, only when visitors came or servants or workmen were in the house did I feel relatively safe.

More housekeepers came and went, but they weren't as mature or kind as Maggie. One exception was an African-American day-helper who was there when I was older. Her touch was gentle and loving, and she helped smooth the way when she could. I remember one housekeeper talking about her religious practice of voodoo. I was fascinated with the connections to the transpersonal realm that were awakened in me by her experiences. Later I would understand it as an underlying religious spirit that we shared, and connecting at this level satisfied a longing to gain access to the spiritual realm. All this was in striking contrast to my family's everyday distant interactions, and it filled my hungry soul.

My mother had been the intellectual one of the family. She had studied the classics and had done some writing of her own, although none of it was kept — not even her library — after her death. When I was old enough to ask about the few books that had remained on the shelf, my father would reach for one book, Gods' Man.[15] Then he would make his lap available for me to climb upon and narrate for me what was clearly his favorite story. His sharing it with me and the contents of the book itself made a profound impression on my psyche.

The book was made up solely of a series of woodcuts; the reader tells the story that he interprets from the pictures. Within our warm embrace my father would interpret the pictures to me, and they had a deep and lasting influence. The story was of an artist's Faustian pact with Death, a figure disguised by a mask, and the painful life he leads following this ominous event. The tale was a commentary on the murky, unredeemed psyche. I absorbed more of the story's meaning with every reading. I was too young to understand its disturbing messages, not least of which was the inappropriateness of my father reading such a narrative to me. This was not a book for a father to read to his young child as it was shrouded in death and hopelessness. I didn't register this at the time. I was mainly intrigued with the pictures and how the relationships unfolded. Most important of all, my father was choosing me to receive a story of such importance to him. My happiness was in sharing his beloved text. It was only later that I realized the enormous impact it had.

Early in the story, following his pact and subsequent success as a budding artist, the protagonist meets an entrepreneur who sets him up with a woman. The turning point in the book comes when he sees a dollar sign tattooed on her body and realizes that she is a whore (fig. 1). (I don't remember how my father explained what a whore was, but I got the idea.) Soon after he discovers this unbearable reality, the artist is thrown in jail. He escapes and is driven out of the city by a mob. He has a brief reprieve with a wife and a child, and then Death returns to claim him.

The theme of darkness accompanying new beginnings is recurrent in this book. The artist launching into his independent, creative life meets darkness directly in the mask of Death, the entrepreneur, the whore, the prison, and the overall betrayal that the tattoo symbolizes. He is held hostage by the shadows of his interior life, which are also manifested in his exterior life.

My father identified with Gods' Man because Death came to the book's protagonist after an encounter with a nurturing wife, just as

Fig. 1: *Tattoo on the shoulder of the model/prostitute. Reprinted from* Gods' Man: A Novel in Woodcuts *by Lynd Ward: New York, Jonathan Cape and Harrison Smith, 1929, © Lynd Ward, renewed by Nanda N. Ward and Robin Ward Savage, by permission of Nanda N. Ward and Robin Ward Savage.*

had happened in his own life with my mother. I independently identified with *Gods' Man*. The story reinforced my already well-entrenched fear that entering life resulted in abandonment, disappointment and death. It reinforced the circumstances of my birth and early life. The book said, "Death will come back to get you; there is no way out." I later established a deeper parallel. I was as shocked at the development of my scars as was the innocent artist at the appearance of the tattoo on the woman's shoulder.

My scars remained the focal point of activity around me. As my father and stepmother were preoccupied with the next treatment plan, I was preoccupied with the humiliation of having the disfiguring scars. I was haunted by the question of what I had done wrong that had brought these scars into being. Developing unsightly keloids had created another wound for me.

When I went to the dermatologist's office with my stepmother, I felt swallowed up with concern about what would happen. Could the doctor fix my arms? Would the x-ray or the dry ice treatments be painful? My stepmother's anxiety was revealed in her pejorative comments about my discomfort. There was no room for discussion about these matters. I was not to exhibit any curiosity or interest in what was happening beyond getting dressed and being ready to go. She didn't want to be reminded of painful realities or embarrassed in front of her friends. So I tried very hard to be good in ways she expected me to be.

My stepmother hovered when the doctor looked at my scars. I wished that I could talk to him by myself and be my own person without her. But she was right there, giving me intimidating looks. I was frozen in her presence, and it seemed as if the disfiguring scars were all there was of me. My unanswered questions remained inside. My stepmother had me wait in another room while she talked to the doctor in private. I imagined she was confirming my fantasies of being hopelessly disfigured for life and remarking on the consequences. One thought came to me — she was confirming her assumption that I could never have a child because it could cause keloids. The scars had made me a pariah. I was never to live normally because of them.

Several years after the scars emerged, I was standing in line at a day camp when the girls in front of me began speculating about what caused warts. I froze. I thought they were talking about me. I felt not only that I was like the ugly toad they were laughing about, but I also worried that other people who touched me might get my warts. I wanted to disappear so that I could avoid the inevitable questions and sneers. I believed that the children's judgment replicated my stepmother's, and their whispered comments devoured what little self-worth I had. This ultimately led to my doctor's suggestion that I have the scars removed. Other medical procedures to reduce the size of the scars had been unsuccessful.

My father and I went to New York to consult a nationally renowned dermatologist about the planned surgery to remove the scars. I was ten years old, and this doctor was the first person in my experience to connect in a genuine way with my feelings about the scars. When I showed him my arms, his warm and immediate response was, "My, you do have a problem, don't you!" His kindness was restorative. In his calm approach and gentle manner he demonstrated an authentic interest in the psychological issues that confronted me; he was more concerned about the psychological effect of having scars than the potential outcome of the surgery. He told me about a little boy who had only one leg and who went to the beach with his friends; he didn't stay behind because of his amputation. The doctor could tell that I was suffering from the humiliation of having the scars. I knew what he was hoping to convey by telling me this story, but my reluctance to expose my scars was deep and unchanging.

I returned home, and in the middle of my fifth grade school year, I underwent the surgery. I had great hopes of being relieved of my burden and being like "all the other girls," wearing sleeveless dresses and moving about more freely. But several weeks after the operation, the scars grew back larger than before. I was devastated.

My stepmother fueled my shame by her response to the keloids. Her rejecting attitude, especially about the scars, had a deep impact on my feelings about myself. Whenever I got undressed at home she quickly left the room. When we went shopping, my stepmother kept salesladies out of the dressing areas so they wouldn't discover my hidden secret. Whenever I changed clothes in front of my friends, I had to plan how to keep my naked arms out of plain view. My stepmother encouraged me to cover the scars at all costs.

When I received a negligee as a high school graduation gift, my stepmother immediately took it to her room and sewed a heavy fabric inside the see-through mesh sleeves. I stood silently by, wondering if she ever imagined my getting into bed naked and exposed — what then? My stepmother's feelings of inferiority inflamed my own. Behind her mask of power, her own shame was stirred. All this was fertile ground for her feelings of insecurity to be projected onto me. I had taken in her repulsion at the scars, and I identified with her fears and rejection of my imperfect body. They made me feel leprous and inferior. Her rejection was another form of abandonment. My plaintive cry was unremitting: Mother, where are you! Why aren't you here to help me?

The keloids made visible the continuing shame and guilt I felt because of my mother's death. They revealed the emotional chaos that was increasing inside me. It was as if the scars on my body formed permanent tears, for there was no safe place to shed the real ones. The scars came from a source inside that I didn't understand, and it raised my curiosity about their origins. If these scars didn't happen to most people, why were they happening to me?

The only course of action remaining was to return to the local dermatologist for dry ice and additional radiation treatments in the hopes of controlling the scars' ultimate size. On my initial visit after the keloids had returned, the doctor showed me pictures from his medical library of a woman with huge keloids on her earlobes that developed after her ears were pierced. While I stared at the shocking photographs of the deforming keloids, I was both captivated and terrified. It was small comfort that someone else in the world had scars like mine, and it instilled in me an even greater fear of what could happen if my skin were cut again. That concern was the doctor's intention in showing me the disturbing photographs.

When I became a teenager, the aversion to revealing my scars intensified. I was unwilling to join my friends when they gathered around the swimming pool in our local park. I wouldn't wear a bathing suit and expose my arms. What I did instead was in part an adolescent rebellion, and it may have arisen from my first dream about the snakes. There was a local zoo near the swimming pool, and there I spent my spare time. Unexpectedly, I was offered a chance to work in the snake pit and display nonpoisonous snakes to the park visitors. The snakes didn't frighten me half as much as showing my scars did. This was a tentative effort to take hold of my state of affairs and later to make an active relationship to the unconscious that the snake represented, but I didn't know that at the time.

Although my father was deeply affected by my suffering, he was unable to diminish my isolation. He could not take a decisive stand against the harmful behavior of my stepmother. But he felt the need for his children to experience a healthier environment, and with prompting from a thoughtful relative, he insisted that my sister and I go away to summer camp. Being away from home for two months and living in the outdoors was a panacea for me, but the required activities involved revealing my scars. When we went swimming in the lake I would run down from the cabin with my hands over my scars in an attempt to save face, but this only roused the scoffing and whispers of the campers. It was all I could do to contain my feelings of hurt and fear of future encounters that would repeat this painful scenario. Yet the overall experience there was quite healing, and unlike the other children who cried on the train going to camp, my sister and I would cry on the train coming back.

As I progressed through high school, I began to doubt myself increasingly. I didn't want to be different from my friends and bring attention to myself. Further rejection was more than I could bear. I sensed I was different but I couldn't accept that reality, so I strove to fit into the group and to find a place outside my stepmother's reach. My father tried to help. Because of his concern that my self-image was declining under the weight of my stepmother's rummage sale attitude about buying things for me, he took me to a fashionable store for my sixteenth birthday to purchase whatever I desired. I bought a short leather coat for thirty dollars. It was the first time I can remember shopping with the freedom to buy something retail, and it made me feel normal. I will never forget it.

In my last years of high school, I had the psychological space and time to reflect on the dynamic of my interactions with my father and stepmother, especially around their reactions to the scars and the effect they had on me. What transpired around this time beautifully illustrated their individual psychology as it interfaced with my own. I sensed that my father was worried that nobody would marry me because of the scars. I asked him outright if that was what he was troubled about. He was so impressed that I would be direct enough to ask that he commented on my forthright expression. In that moment his respect for me became evident, and that did more for me than the nature of his concern itself.

My stepmother's reaction to my forthrightness was quite different. One day the realization came to me that soon I would be leaving home, and this was the last chance I would have to talk to her about her rejecting attitude toward the scars. I gathered the strength to describe how it had made me feel when she left the room any time that I was undressed. She denied doing any of the things I pointed out and said it was all in my imagination. Initially I felt disappointed and alone with my own experience. Then I felt the rage that I had long suppressed. Eventually I was able to see her dismissal of me as her inability to accept her own limitations and behaviors. I knew from that interchange that an honest relationship with her would never be possible and that I would have to work on the meaning of the scars on my own.

During the summer before my senior year in high school an event occurred that, in hindsight, I see as beginning the process that would lead to that work. One afternoon I was sitting in the living room with my father when suddenly there was a loud crash just outside on our quiet residential street. Naturally it shocked us, and we went out to see what had happened. Some teenagers driving up the street had run into a parked car. In the back seat of their car was a young woman from my school who had the most beautiful cameo-like face I had ever seen. In the accident her face was badly cut. She eventually had plastic surgery that successfully repaired her facial wounds, but the event set off a chain of endless discussions in our family about how that accident would have been "a disaster" if it had happened to me.

This added to my anxiety about being scarred in a place that could not be hidden, as the scars on my upper arms could be. For a long time after this event I was obsessed with horrible images of being grossly disfigured, and the fear almost kept me from leaving the house. Yet the psyche had something else in store for me as a result of that accident. The girl who was hurt went on to college, and at the urging of her father, a dermatologist, she became a speech therapist. One day my father suggested that speech therapy would be a good field for me to explore. A new possibility for leaving the dark state of affairs was beginning to emerge, but it would unfold slowly and, as I would come to understand, would be born out of the darkness itself. Here is how it evolved.

After a battery of academic tests, the high school counselors announced that I probably wouldn't succeed in higher education. I had hoped that they would recognize that my poor performance was due, in part, to my woeful home environment and my psychological state at that time. But I knew that in spite of my poor scores, I had to get away from home. Somehow I found the inner strength to apply to college, an action that changed my life dramatically.

Although she didn't support my leaving, when I insisted, my step-mother suggested I apply to the university near her hometown in another state. I was accepted. At that university, what could have been merely an extension of my life with her in fact contained the promise of a transformation. My faculty advisor in the speech therapy department turned out to be a Jungian psychologist. Within a few weeks, I had my first exposure to Jung's writings and was shown a conceptual framework of the psyche through which I could undertake my investigation into the scars' role in my psychological makeup. Therein began my first conscious awareness of the process of individuation that was alive inside me. I found a way of viewing the psyche that could help me begin to make sense of my early experiences. Jung's approach included the spiritual element that could contain my suffering. My path was being presented to me in all its depth of meaning. Here was the rescue, born out of an apparently hopeless situation of being subjected to this particular stepmother. From the core of the pain had come the source of the healing.

CHAPTER TWO

# THE SCARS BLOSSOM AND ANALYSIS BEGINS

*Contact with the unconscious opens the prison which we have made*
*for ourselves with our conscious views and ego-bound aims, and at*
*the same time an analogous process takes place in the unconscious*
*psyche: through the application of conscious insight the unconscious*
*is freed from its irreducible, unchanging quality, and is altered by*
*contact with the understanding consciousness.*[16]

Before any new psychological discoveries could make an impact on
my everyday life, I had to deal with the adjustment of entering college
and the world of new relationships and unfamiliar surroundings. The
inner turmoil and chaos stirred once again at this new beginning, and
I felt very alone. During the first few months of living in the dorm, I
met a fellow student that I liked and admired, and we decided to be
roommates. She came from a refined and cultured family that, as she
described it, sounded like my own family before I was born. The relationship couldn't last under all my hopes and projections. Shortly after
our decision to room together, she unexpectedly changed her mind
and went off to room with someone else. I felt desolate. My hurt and
disappointment at being abandoned by her affected my body immediately. A rash of keloids appeared spontaneously across my chest. I was
horrified that the scars could come up spontaneously as a public
expression of my sorrow when there had been no physical injury
to cause them.

Shortly thereafter I became conscious of the underlying depression
that I had been suppressing most of my life. This brutal rejection and
the new scars' appearance finally brought it to the surface. I began to
think that the inner guiding spirit that was beginning to awaken in
me had decided to abandon me once again, for I had projected my
own guiding spirit onto the abandoning friend. When this spiritual
crisis was at its zenith, I wondered if I had the courage to live.

After my depression had lifted enough for me to take action, I traveled to Atlanta to visit yet another renowned dermatologist. I hoped

that medical research had uncovered a new solution to keloid scar formation. The doctor diagnosed the scars on my chest as "acne keloids," but he had no treatment to offer me. He could only warn me not to touch or self-treat any future acne that I might experience as it could precipitate more scarring.

Even though I had an active social life and lived in a sorority that offered me camaraderie, my concern about the development of the scars was paramount. The proliferating scars on my chest meant that now I had more keloids to cover up. I was becoming aware that the scars were not going to go away and that new ones could be in the offing. A persistent force was living inside me, insisting on making its presence known, and I experienced this force as out of control. The emerging scars were visible evidence of it. Once again I sought medical help, but no treatment was available.

For my academic major, I had chosen speech therapy. My advisor, who introduced me to Jungian thought, taught the first required course, "The Psychological Processes of Speech Therapists." This was a new beginning I could welcome, one in which darkness would be made conscious through the exploration of our inner worlds. It was in working with the unconscious that I would discover how traumatized I had been by the development of the scars. This realization came about during a role-playing session. We took turns playing the part of the child-patient and therapist. When it was my turn to be the child, I drew a picture of the airplane that I had taken to New York when I went with my father to consult the dermatologist. The warmth in the play therapy relationship elicited the memory of the warmth of the doctor's empathic response, and I was quite open when I told my "therapist" this narrative. Discussing the scars was discussing the trauma of my childhood and brought it ever closer to my consciousness. But when it came time to present the drawings to our whole class for review and feedback, something quite different happened.

Each of us took turns discussing what had transpired in our individual play time, and with my permission, my therapist showed the drawings I had done. I was supposed to talk about what the pictures meant to me, but when I looked at the image of the airplane my mind went blank. I could not for the life of me remember what the drawing was about. Everyone grew silent and waited for me to say something. My heart started pounding rapidly. I burst into tears and ran out of the room. After that traumatic event, I became conscious of just how much

I had both denied and repressed my feelings about the scars and about having others see them.

Several years later, this fear was realized. As I came out of the sorority house where I was living at the time, I slipped on the stairs and cut my knee. As I was recovering, I could see that a keloid was beginning to form on the wound. This scar would not be so easy to hide. It would further limit what I could wear, and I was greatly alarmed. The medical profession couldn't help me, but an inspiration came to me. I went to a good friend who had experience with healing rituals. Her response was immediate. We sat together in her office, her hand on my knee, and she conducted a private healing meditation. It was a very powerful moment, and during it, an image of God was invoked in me like an epiphany. The unwanted keloid on my knee did not materialize.

With this healing I realized I could have some control over the emergence of the keloid if the conditions and my attitude were "just right." My friend as guide had helped initiate me into the spiritual level of my psyche and its influence on the body. The power to arrest the growth of the unwanted keloid came from prayer. This was the first opportunity for me to openly express a significant part of my nature, the spiritual dimension. It allowed me to connect consciously to the God-image inside myself and to get a faint glimmer of God's reflection in the scars.

I was naive and immature at this time, and control over the emergence of the keloid went to my head. I thought: "I'll get rid of all my scars that way." I went so far as to gather a few of my colleagues and my friend who had performed the earlier ritual. But as might be expected, the ritual didn't work. It felt wrong as soon as we started, and I called it off. Grace, I learned, comes only when the moment is ripe, when the psyche is supporting it, and when the reason is compelling. Furthermore, my relationship with God had to be developed in an individual setting, not in a collective one.

The psyche seemed intent that I understand the initiation aspect of this new development. It sent me a milestone dream.

*I am wearing a gown that has only one shoulder strap.*
*My keloids have turned into flowers and have created the other strap.*

I awoke with an indescribable excitement and a great sense of awe. This was the first dream I had about the keloids and the first confirmation that the keloid could mean anything other than a physical deformity. Its implication was far-reaching, and it would take me half a lifetime to integrate its depth of meaning. The dream was showing me a new beginning in the form of the flower, a symbol for rebirth, arising from the body's fertile territory where the scars themselves arose.

The keloid turning into a flower suggested that I could dispel the feeling that I was unworthy and the ever-present temptation to think of myself as inferior, the feeling I had lived with all my life as an orphan. My inspiration to approach the scar in a meditation meant psychologically that I recognized a living connection to the Self as significant to healing. The Self was behind my small and tentative ego, inspiring me like the nurturing mother I longed for.

As a young woman I wanted to be found attractive, and I associated that with wearing a strapless evening gown. The psyche presented the keloid flower in this context so that I might reflect upon the source of the pain as the source of potential healing, as if to say, "Your wish can be granted, and it will come from within, from what you already have inside you. The suffering in your life carries the hidden treasure."

My individuation would require integrating the inferior side of myself that the keloid represented into an authentic experience of the Self, the flower that blooms. The dream told me that my life would not be limited to suffering and meaninglessness; the Self had something else in store. Pursuing my interest in the keloid would lead to a greater realization of my wholeness, of my flowering. Jung said, "The flower is . . . like a friendly sign, a numinous emanation from the unconscious, showing the dreamer . . . where he can find the seed that wants to sprout in him too."[17] The keloid and the autonomous life force it represented were that seed. With the flower dream, I felt for the first time the possibility that I could heal, I could "flower," that there was hope for my feeling life to be experienced consciously. The scar's potential for transformation into something "as beautiful as a flower" was my hoped-for psychological transformation.

As I was finishing my senior year in college and the potential "new birth" of graduation was before me, my father died. He had told me he wanted to wait for me to become independent before he left. That was now happening. He felt it was his job to take care of his children until they were launched into life. The symbol of this independence for him was my getting a car. The day after I bought my first car, when he felt his goal had been accomplished, he died. He had stayed around far beyond what he would have preferred.

With his death I felt forlorn. My father had been the vital impetus to my achieving independence and to stretching myself intellectually. Moreover, he had been my first and primary love. I was bereft, and I grieved his loss enormously. I feared I wouldn't have the resolve to go forward into life without his support.

But by then I had discovered Jung and had made the initial steps toward connecting consciously to my psychological process. That was the foundation I needed. I was beginning to understand conceptually what was happening to me psychologically. It was as if I had found another father who understood my experience and offered a new lap in which I could heal and gather strength.

Now I needed an analyst who could help me implement Jung's work. After I finished my master's degree at the university, I moved to Los Angeles. It seemed the gods were looking out for me. Within a few weeks I found a job in the public school system as a speech therapist, a highly sought-after position others had been waiting months to get. My fantasy of myself as an "independent working girl in the big city" was to become a reality. I was finally going to have a home within which I could explore my inner life.

As soon as I arrived in Los Angeles I made an appointment with a Jungian analyst. One of the first dreams that came to me then offered an image of my ongoing psychological state and a way to proceed with my analytic work.

> *I was imprisoned in a tower and was sitting on the upper balcony, painting at an easel.*
> *A thought came to me: if I could paint I would always be free.*

My fear was that I was put inside the tower as a punishment for being born and causing my mother's death. The image of the tower, in contrast, suggested that the analytic setting was like a prison tower to which I was voluntarily relegating myself, not for a punishing confinement but as a necessary containment for a psychological rebirth. Through this dream the psyche was trying to give me the courage and the tenacity to rescue the core of my existence from its imprisonment in the mother/death complex, to rescue me from the prison of my own distress.

The image of being in the tower posed the question: did my mother's death mean I would inherit the kingdom (represented by the symbol of the tower) or be banished from it? With my stepmother's arrival, this question had been answered. I was banished. Now, another question arose: was the psychological experience of being banished from the kingdom irreversible, or could it change?

Through analysis I began a purposeful regression into the unconscious and into my past. I began to relive and make conscious my fate, my mother's death at my birth, and its effect on my inner life. Confined in the analytic tower, I became further acquainted with the darkness within me. My mother and father, representing the "original unity" in my psyche, had reigned in a kingdom of culture and society. With my birth, life in that kingdom came to an abrupt end. I was separated from the "main house" my mother represented and was relegated to the prison tower just outside where, I felt certain, the rest of humanity would find me guilty as charged. It was a tower of deep isolation.

With my mother's death my family lost the object of its adoration and got me instead. The magnificent kingdom from which I had been excluded, a life with my mother, carried the projection of the Self, the totality of my personality. I lived in its shadow. The most poignant aspect of the tower dream was the offering of a way to find an active connection to the Self. The dream said that painting could access the deep interior world. Responding to that important piece of information, my analyst suggested that I begin to paint spontaneous images. I went to an art class to acquaint myself with the materials and took to painting instantly. It was as if the unconscious had been waiting for me. Colors, forms and shapes of which I had no idea were forthcoming. Giving birth to these images gave birth to the unconscious as it gave birth to me. The discipline of painting gave me a new sense of freedom as the dream had predicted. If this would lead to a psychological rebirth and living out of my own authority, then I could inhabit my own kingdom.

During this period I painted a collage of my dream of the keloids turning into flowers (fig. 2). In the painting my dress was black, and the multitude of black flowers scattered about represented my inner condition (my complexes and attitudes that needed to be analyzed and worked on). The keloids were manifestations of the darkness that had come from both inside and outside and had lodged in my body. As a symbol, the black rose has been said to convey the silence of the

Figure 2: *A collage of my dream of the keloids turning into flowers.*

initiate, and through my art I was engaging silently in an initiation process that could lead to transformation.

I did many multimedia works of art with the scars as a theme (fig. 3). One series of paintings showed the keloids' dynamic participation in the process of transformation. They exemplified the psychological principles with which I was working. Without my conscious intention, the first series of four paintings revealed the element of light hidden within the darkness. In the first painting of the series I wanted to create the birth umbilicus and the containment it represented and that I had missed. These paintings have a high relief like the scars themselves. Next I portrayed the umbilicus breaking up into little pieces resembling flowers, scattered pieces of the original container. The third painting contained these pieces, now enlarged and in their dark tumultuous aspects. All three of these paintings reflected how the keloids expressed the psyche and the circumstances that evolved after the original container had been broken. In the fourth the light emerges. Each time I painted, I was reliving the six days I had with my mother when the spirit was alive and the eternal was manifest.

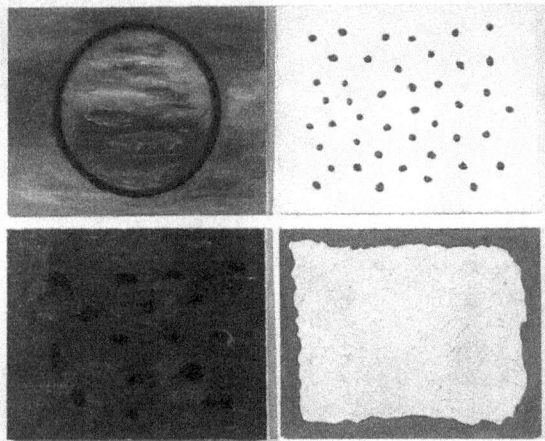

Figure 3: *Series of four paintings revealing the light hidden within the darkness.*

Painting kept me close to the umbilicus from which I was cut too soon. In doing this artwork I was expressing myself from the inside out, just as the scars did, and I was creating a psychological umbilicus that connected the ego to the unconscious.

Having a means of expressing myself from the depths was just the medicine I needed. Painting took me to deeper levels of the psyche, and that engendered in me a sense that I had something of value that lived inside and that wanted to express itself. While I was painting I felt the sense of security I had been longing for, and I gained the reassurance that I was not alone. Retrieving images I didn't know existed inside me until they appeared on the canvas helped me to create the containment I needed.

The world of my mother reached up to me as the "inner other" I longed to have as a partner. It was like having a mother who looks lovingly at her child and gives that child the courage to develop. Having missed this experience, I discovered that the inner world can still provide it.

The orphan in me was no longer so lonely, since I was experiencing the unconscious in such a vital way. The inner world was where my mother lived in me, and now I had found a way of hearing her. The dreams, visions, and inspirations all came from my mother's world, the immortal part of me. What I needed was a closeness with whatever represented the eternal. It would be the only satisfying link from my daily life to my mother's world.

Analysis was helping me understand my psychology at ever deeper levels. Exploring the personal layer of my psychology helped me further define my behavior, my complexes, my relationship to others and to the Self. But the paintings touched the deepest layer of all. They came from the most distant nonverbal core of my being, fueling the fires of my transformation.

My analytic work was initiated by the scars and required intense solitary concentration. Residence in the analytic tower gave me the opportunity to incubate. Incubation is the first stage of initiation. The unfolding of my transformation could follow from that. Living in the tower of the psyche is a lonely existence, but acknowledging and accepting my orphan reality would make it possible to become my own person. The challenge was to make the tower my temple.

A year and a half into my analysis and my life as a single woman in the workplace, I met the man whom I later married. This was a significant turning point and invoked the familiar life-and-death struggle at new beginnings. Chaos stirred in the deep unconscious. My body was inevitably affected, and a few months after our wedding, new keloids grew large upon my right shoulder.

The keloids were born again, coming unexpectedly and affecting me even more than in the past. The new keloids expressed my ever-present fear of new beginnings and what they might bring. The disfiguring scars reflected my anxiety and despair. I felt great anguish over their appearance and powerless before their persistence in my life. Somehow I had thought that defying the predictions that I wouldn't marry because of my scarred body meant that the dark spell was over. I also thought my awakening consciousness through analytic work meant that I had more control over my body. Alas, I was not only in denial of the realities of the life force and its volatile ways, but I had temporarily ignored my newfound knowledge of the power of the unconscious, the value of its expression, and the fact that rescue comes in many forms. The scars were reinforcing these principles, teaching me a lesson about these fundamental truths. It would take many years to decipher what they had to convey.

As we drove back from our honeymoon, it was as if my whole system had shut down; I was numb. The reality of having left my freedom behind and facing the obligation of a committed relationship was now before me. Later I would understand that in fact a greater sense of freedom was in the offing, for I had taken a large step forward and that in itself would give the psyche more room to transform. The scars on my shoulder formed my own personal version of an epaulet. I had made another transition, and they expressed the conflicting forces in my psyche. They were a badge of honor that would require my complete dedication to fully realize. My analysis would have to go deeper yet as the scars were becoming my trademark and my relationship to them was binding.

My feelings about the new scars emerging didn't reach consciousness until I took my husband to meet the three women who were so influential to me in college. One was the woman who introduced me to Jungian work, another was my woman friend who had conducted the healing meditation, and the third was a colleague of theirs. All three had attended the second healing ceremony that I had so abruptly canceled. Now I told them about the scars that had just emerged on my shoulder and, as I was doing so, I dissolved into uncontrollable tears. I was overwhelmed with despair over the scars continuing to appear so unexpectedly and so unstoppably. I was convinced that my body was ignoring the fact that I was trying so hard "to do the right things and be good."

My friends were quite compassionate, and one of them invited me into another room where we could talk alone. I don't remember exactly what she said, but her words consoled me. Our talk was like a meditation, and it calmed me down considerably. I rejoined the others, still sad, yet now with a deeper acceptance of my fate. After some time had passed, I felt that the persistence of the keloids had an important message for me and found the energy to pursue their meaning.

Although being married was a reprieve from the aloneness of the orphan, it didn't rescue me from having to develop my own creativity. The marriage initiated me into intense relationship issues, and one such issue was the painful awareness that I wasn't going to be completely taken care of, as I had hoped to be. I felt abandoned once again, yet by carrying the suffering this created I eventually began to realize I couldn't escape the continuing hard work of individuation. Rather, the suffering was a meaningful part of it.

The scars continued to hold my attention. They inspired my continuing investigation into my psychological life. One dream suggested:

> *The way to investigate the keloid is to*
> *carefully peel off its skin, layer by layer.*

But to investigate its layers meant I had to take a careful inventory of my life's inner and outer activities and their many strata of meaning. This included a thorough understanding of the myth of the "orphan" that I was living, the myth in which this organic symptom was embedded, in order to see the larger dynamic in which the keloid came to life.

During my analysis I was learning about the dynamics of the orphan archetype. The term "orphan" was used by the alchemists to name a unique stone, the "orphan stone," a gem similar to our modern solitaire. The alchemists equated the orphan stone with the Philosopher's Stone, the *lapis*. This stone represents the totality, or "the one;" it corresponds to the psychological idea of the Self. The *lapis* is the stone of the wise, the germ of the individuation process. In one text it is known as the homeless orphan who is slain at the beginning of the alchemical process for purposes of transformation.[18] It is both worthless and precious, the set of opposites familiar to the orphan. I, too, often felt as if I were either the most "inferior one" or the most "superior one."

Jung calls up the orphan archetype in connection with the *lapis*. In *Memories, Dreams, Reflections*[19] he tells of a mistake that was made in the dimensions of the cornerstone of his tower in Bollingen. Jung's mason wanted to send the stone back. Jung immediately felt it was "his" stone and insisted on keeping it. A Latin verse suddenly came to him, a verse which referred to the *lapis* as despised and rejected, and he chiseled it into the stone.[20]

> Here stands the mean, uncomely stone,
> 'Tis very cheap in price!
> The more it is despised by fools,
> The more loved by the wise.

On the third side of the stone, the one facing the lake, he let the stone "speak for itself" and carved these quotations from alchemy (here translated from Latin inscription):

> I am an orphan, alone; nevertheless I am found every-
> where. I am one, but opposed to myself. I am youth
> and old man at one and the same time. I have known
> neither father nor mother, because I have had to be
> fetched out of the deep like a fish, or fell like a white

stone from heaven. In woods and mountains I roam, but I am hidden in the innermost soul of man. I am mortal for everyone, yet I am not touched by the cycle of aeons.[21]

Viewing the orphan as a symbol of the autonomous human being makes it possible to examine the pieces of this "whole" and not get bogged down in the seemingly hopeless web of complexes the orphan faces. Analyzing these pieces is the alchemical "slaying at the beginning of the process." It is what I had to do.

The main set of opposites the orphan has to carry is, on the one hand, being chosen to survive and thus special and, on the other hand, being abandoned and alienated from the source of containment and nourishment and thus inferior, not worthy of a rightful place in life. The abandoned child is the core motif of the orphan archetype, yet the orphan carries the autonomous life force inherent in the psyche, the opposite of abandonment. Buried beneath these dynamics lies the potential for a profound inflation. A negative and positive inflation was constellated in me from my identity as a scapegoat. When I was feeling special, I thought I was entitled to more than my fair share of caring since I had suffered my "allotted" amount of suffering with the initial trauma. The negative inflation resulted from my carrying the guilt and despair my family couldn't carry and incorporating the blame into myself. I henceforth felt guilt and responsibility for causing many of the events that happened around me but that objectively had nothing to do with me. My feelings of guilt were commingled with my feelings of unworthiness. These were the many layers of the orphan dynamic I was beginning to work on.

Guilt is primary in this psychological profile. The orphan feels a fundamental guilt as if condemned by the Self. She feels that the Self (as the mother and as the hostile betrayer) has turned away and that this is a higher judgment for which the orphan must carry the guilt. If guilt continues to fill her existence, it leaves little room for the Self to come into being. This is an archaic guilt, not to be confused with the more conscious guilt one feels when leaving a familiar container (such as a religious belief or the personal family), but more closely akin to the guilt for becoming more conscious and for being alive.

Erich Neumann said that "not-to-be-loved is identical with being abnormal, sick, 'leprous,' and above all 'condemned'."[22] Instead of blaming the world or mankind, the orphan feels guilty. I succumbed to the open arms of this complex of feelings. The loss of my mother dominated my interior life as much as living with my stepmother and getting the scars dominated my exterior one. During the early years of my marriage, I also struggled with my fears of separation, continuing to feel the guilt of the survivor who escaped the clutches of death that had hovered so near, yet had spared me. I lived continually in fear of its return. This combination of fear and guilt led to aggression against myself. In my psychological confusion accidents would happen. I would break something precious or cut myself with a knife. The "accidents" took place when I was separated from my husband, who represented protection and nourishment. I experienced even temporary separations as abandonment. Being left turned into anger against myself. Suicidal tendencies arose from the deep unconscious. I was identifying with the dark inner force, contributing to my guilt and despair. Jung explained it this way: "[H]e carries the enemy within himself — a deadly longing for the abyss, a longing to drown in his own source, to be sucked down to the realm of the Mothers."[23]

When I felt abandoned, these destructive acts against myself were unconscious attempts to beat Death to the draw. In these chaotic moments I was reaching back to a memory of the mother who was so brutally taken away and, perhaps, to a way of merging with her in death. I was unaware of the despair I felt without her, and I denied the pain accompanying it. Deeper still, the subliminal fantasy was: "If I'm hurt, maybe she will come and find me, so I'll create occasions where we can meet." Like most orphans, I became drawn to a death mode rather than a life mode. I did understand at the time that the compulsion to hurt myself contained my deepest sorrow born from the original moment of abandonment. After further study of these dynamics I saw another dimension: *I unconsciously wanted to recreate the original trauma in order to rediscover myself.* That was a far more uplifting thought, and it was one I could work with productively. This realization didn't condone the self-destructive behaviors, but it gave them a redeeming meaning.

A return to the original trauma came up in a tangible way during my early years of analysis. In conjunction with painting I used the sandtray, a tool in therapy where the symbols of the psyche are played out in a sandbox. The player creates images in the sand or chooses from a variety of figures and objects to place in the sand to create a scene. The first scene I created was a symbolic expression of how the unconscious responded to my birth trauma. In the sandtray:

*There had been an accident. An ambulance was on the scene. Emergency crews were there to rescue the injured person.*

Analysis would offer rescue, and if the emergency crew could speak they would have said to me *"Someone died here, and you must believe it."* But I never wanted to believe it. The death of my mother created a wound so profound that it seemed I would never get past it. Rather, I had to go *into* it.

As part of this process, I identified the fairy tale that was most like my particular version of the orphan dynamic. It was "The Little Match Girl" by Hans Christian Andersen.[24] This story is about a poor little girl who sells matches on the street. She is afraid to go home, for she hasn't sold any matches and her father will beat her. In the bitter cold of winter she finds a corner beside a house to curl up in. She strikes a match to keep warm, and in the glow of its flame she fancies she is sitting beside a warm stove. When the flame goes out and the vision vanishes, she strikes another match. With this she sees a bounty of food upon a table with a beautiful tablecloth and fine china. In the light of another match she is sitting in front of a large Christmas tree bedecked with candles. She strikes her last matches, and in a halo of light her dead grandmother appears, looking so gentle and happy. She cries out to her grandmother, "Oh, do take me with you." The next morning she is found frozen to death, in the corner between the houses, with rosy cheeks and a smile on her face.

Like the Little Match Girl, I had encountered the dark side of life. The positive side took up residence in fantasies in which I longed for my mother to return. This left me on the outside looking in at the warmth of life I imagined others possessed and was a psychological form of death because I was not living my own life. Looking out from the interior window of the psyche, the orphan longs for whatever others have, from literal objects to their creative endeavors. Yearning for others' accomplishments is a way of avoiding the hard work of developing one's own potential. What one desires in others is an unlived aspect in oneself that needs attending. Failing to accept the orphan fate sets the stage for envy, leading one to make unconscious demands that others compensate for what one didn't get. Some part of me was like the Little Match Girl, frozen in time, losing the strength to hold on. Warmth seemed short-lived, and the wish for the return of the "grand" mother haunted me.

Many years into my marriage, the fantasy of reunion with my mother surfaced in a palpable way. One night when my husband was late coming home from work, the fantasy bounded out of the unconscious and stunned me. I imagined that he was bringing my mother home as a surprise. My emotions were completely engaged in this image, as if it were a realistic expectation. When I reflected on the fantasy, I realized how unconscious I had been of the pervasiveness of my orphan complex and the loneliness and fear that I was feeling. Right beneath my everyday existence, in one form or another, the desire for my mother was always there. The longing for her was real and was mixed in with death, just as the longing for the grandmother was for the Little Match Girl. For many years it seemed as if the good mother was nowhere to be found, but I continued to look for her. I realized that this tale and this desire for my mother was behind the childhood play with my sister, when I was the poor widow on the street coming into her house of finery. I projected the mother wherever there was a individual or a group that seemed to offer what I felt I had missed.

The scars intensified my feelings of being deprived of the good and protective mother and made me want to be included in all activities that represented the mothering I imagined others had. If there was a large gathering or a one-on-one conversation, I wanted to be there. There was no end to what I imagined the mother to be, and wherever she was, that was where I wanted to be. Everyone was a mother from whom I wanted to be reborn. A friendly gesture was a mother with whom I wanted to stay. I followed each person back into themselves, all the while hoping to fill the empty center of myself. I fell headlong into a deprivation complex.

The scars were born from this deep feeling of deprivation, and what I didn't understand at the time was that the body was helping me carry it. Analyzing the many layers of the keloid, I came to appreciate how much the scars had protected me from my stepmother, because she distanced herself from their disfiguring aspects. Nevertheless, at a feeling level, everyone else seemed like the psychological skin that I needed for protection. I had been initiated into darkness at my beginnings, but I hadn't accepted it. It would take me years to integrate the fact that darkness inevitably accompanies a new birth. In the meantime, I was afraid to live my own life outside the psychological atmosphere of loss, a life without my mother. Fear of being alone meant fear of being myself. The fear resurfaced whenever there was a constellation of the mother leaving.

In his book, *The Child*, Erich Neumann wrote: "Once we appreciate the positive significance of the child's total dependency on the primal relationship, we cannot be surprised by the catastrophic effects that ensue when that relationship is disturbed or destroyed."[25] My psyche crystallized around the numinous moment of my mother's death. My ego needed to experience it over and over again to reawaken the necessary courage to go on. With each descent, whether psychological (depression), physiological (the scars) or purposeful (analytic work), I returned to that initial time. If I could resist the temptation to unconsciously act out the complexes, returning there could become a rebirth. If my psyche had not desired transformation and I had not supported the individuation process, I could have gone the way of the Little Match Girl. The pull toward death was an aspect of my orphan dynamic. It had been reinforced in my reading of *Gods' Man*, but fortunately was balanced by *Wee Fishie Wun* which carried the hope for renewal, for transforming the darkness into gold.

CHAPTER THREE

# TRANSFORMING THE DARKNESS INTO GOLD

*The real meaning and purpose of symbol production . . .*
*is to bring about an awareness of those primordial images*
*that belong to all men and can therefore lead the individual out of*
*his isolation . . . . for healing comes only from what leads*
*[one] beyond himself and beyond his entanglement in the ego.*[26]

The early experience of abandonment intensifies the dynamic that makes new beginnings in later life a constant threat of destruction from within. What is newly born brings in its opposite — that which will threaten it with extinction. This is the danger for the orphan who must struggle consciously with these barriers to new life.

As I explored how I was living out the archetype of the orphan, a dream symbol helped me see the connection between the scars and my orphan psychology. The night after I had been putting together some material on the scars to present in a seminar, to my astonishment a dream said:

*I was giving a talk about frogs.*

For many years I felt like a frog because of the keloids on my skin. The disfiguring scars were symbolic of the initial darkness, the unbidden, chaotic material of the body from which the opus begins to unfold. But out of this darkness is born the light. This dynamic holds true for the orphan who leans toward death, for renewal becomes possible in that lowest moment. The dream illuminated this psychological dynamic — that what is considered the "lower" element, the "concrete" side of things, if understood symbolically, holds the promise of transformation. The frog is a good symbol for this. It is an amphibian, hatched in water as a tadpole and transformed into an air-breathing adult. The fairy tale *"The Frog Prince"*[27] graphically illustrates the symbol of the frog's transformation. For many years there was an unformed, embryonic aspect to my own psychology, and the yet-to-be-revealed "superior" part of myself was buried inside. The scars represented the inferior frog aspects and the repulsiveness I felt myself to have. They covered a host of shadow aspects in myself, inferior qualities as well as superior ones.

It is a challenge to accept one's imperfections and let them be a guide, and this was exactly what unfolded with the keloids. Shakespeare refers to this, using the image of the toad, and to accepting the despised parts of oneself to bring about their transformation.

> Sweet are the uses of adversity,
> Which like the toad, ugly and venomous,
> Wears yet a precious jewel in his head . . . .[28]

As a symbol of transformation, the frog exemplifies the promise of renewal. It represents the dark primordial aspect one carries deep within, and at the same time it is one's potential wholeness. Jung commented on the frog symbol in the *Visions Seminar*:

> We are the repulsive, ugly husks surrounding
> the golden kernel, the divine soul of man . . . .
> [It is man's] 'nothing-but' aspect . . . . that is only
> the outer shell . . . [out of which] the beautiful
> man is liberated . . . . The thing that is ugly and
> repulsive is precisely what leads to redemption
> . . . . [It is] [n]ot perfection of man but his
> imperfection [that] is meant.[29]

This undeniable fact was stirring in my psyche but was not consciously articulated as I did a second series of paintings of the scars. It was only later that I saw their relevance to these themes. In this series I began with the red scar (fig. 4). In the second painting, water emerged out of the scar. The undervalued and despised bursts forth and begins to live. This represented the flow of inner waters in the unconscious and in the keloid as symbol. In the third painting the water fertilized the ground for the yet-unborn parts of myself to come into being. It was like Noah's flood that led to death and then to rebirth. Since the keloid was a divine phenomenon for me from the beginning, the water surging forth from it was like divine water, the nourishment in the unconscious that the orphan seeks. The final painting was a star made up of a multiplicity of small gold squares:

Fig. 4: *Water emerging out of the red scar fertilizes the unborn parts of myself.*

my totality. The star symbolizes guiding qualities. This was an inner star, a guiding light, just as the keloids were. The beginning of creation, the *prima materia* (first or primary matter), is the original material of life. My keloids were the *prima materia*. They represented the new beginning of my unique and individual personality and ultimately became a star for me.

The star would come to me again in a totally unexpected way. The seeds for its second appearance began with my transition from working for five years as a speech therapist in the school system to a position in a child guidance center as a licensed counselor. In this new role I could give full expression to my deep interest in the psyche and integrate it freely into my professional life. Finally established in the career I loved, I began for the first time to feel more settled not only professionally but emotionally. That laid a more solid foundation for continued transformation and for another transition in life when I would be challenged once again.

My husband expressed a strong desire to have a child. Despite my increasing confidence, I had been avoiding discussions about becoming pregnant. A familiar fear gripped me unceasingly. The fear had many levels, the deepest of which was my resistance to creating new life and, although not consciously formed at the time, the fear that a literal death could accompany the actual birth. I could not visualize myself being a mother and, with my own child, reliving the early years that were so

Fig. 5: *Clay mermaid.*

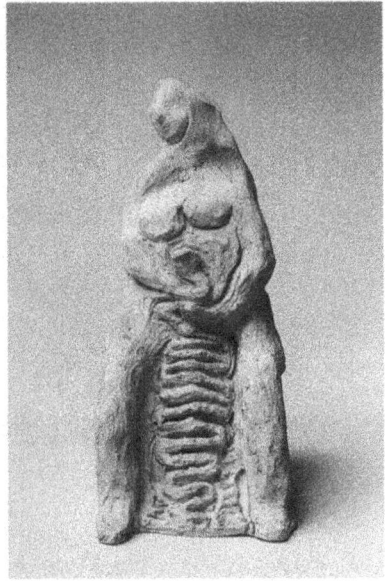

Fig. 6: *The snake.*

Figs. 7–8: *Religious figures.*

painful for me. Also frightening was the risk of creating more keloidal growth at the site of an episiotomy or caesarean section. My stepmother had warned me about this possibility, and her anxiety over the scars and childbirth stirred again inside me. I did not honestly believe I could be a source of healthy new life.

I incubated this dilemma for quite a while, knowing that something beyond my ego would have to intervene to help me. One thought emerged to move me along. I became aware that, as an orphan, I felt that the continuum of life stopped with my mother's death. I hadn't been able to see myself as contributing to the continuation of life. Then I considered that perhaps I was ethically compelled to do so. I also wanted to preserve my marriage, and I knew that if I didn't pre-pare myself psychologically to accept this new responsibility within its framework, I probably would have difficulty conceiving. So I decided to make a conscious and deliberate descent into my psyche in order to cultivate the soil for a conception.

As if instinctively preparing a nest, I cleared out a small clothes clos-et and built a wide shelf inside its borders. For three months I sat for hours at a time in my private sanctuary engaging in active imagination using clay. As I called up the creative energies within me, the nourish-ing mother image, so absent in my conscious psyche, became activat-ed. I was ushering in new life, and by shaping the formless clay and carving out the figures that began to emerge, I was reshaping myself into a new person from the inside out — one who would be strong enough to carry another life. At the end of the series of many small clay figurines, the foundation was successfully laid, and I conceived.

The first clay image I made during this period was of a mermaid (fig. 5). It represented my insufficiently developed ego and explained why my fears were so great. My ego was still in the fish stage. After making the mermaid, my psyche returned to this early phase of evo-lution, and the following images were mostly of animals. The snake came up repeatedly. Several figures were embracing the snake (fig. 6).

As I descended further, religious images began to emerge (figs. 7–8). This level of the psyche led to a surprising development that appeared in the next figure, a reclining woman with her hand on her knee (fig. 9). When that figure presented itself unexpectedly, it was a few minutes before I realized that the unconscious wanted me to recall the spiritual ritual I had done for the keloid on my knee and the healing result. By presenting the image to me, the psyche was saying,

"Remember what happened with the keloid on your knee. Once again you are in the prayer moment, making it real by doing a healing ritual in clay." This reminded me that the presence of God was behind me, and with this insight the next image came into being. It was a figure of the Self holding my ego in its arms, as it had done in response to my prayer meditation (fig. 10).

With the support of the Self, a series of masculine and feminine couples followed (figs. 11–12); a conception took place, and then the birth (fig. 13). This last clay figure was the second significant turning point in the series, and it was the most difficult to finish. As it was coming to life I felt it wanted to show me just how deeply I really did want a baby, both literally and psychologically. In anticipation of a new adaptation, I had been quite frightened to let this birth happen. I bolted out of the closet and ran around the house, going from room to room in an agitated state. Minutes later I realized what I was anxious about: the fear of new life and what attended it. Only then was I able to go back to the clay and finish it. It was hard to accept having something good, like the birth of a child, happen to me.

With this particular figurine, the unconscious led me to make a literal image of birth so that I could feel the pull of new life surrounding a birth experience. I needed the psychological experience of the birth in order to have the confidence to become a mother myself. A clay piece of a mother and child followed, a reassurance that life could be lived and celebrated (fig. 14).

When I did the final standing figure (fig. 15), I immediately knew I had completed the series. The transition from the mermaid at the beginning to the full-bodied woman at the end indicated that sufficient change and development had taken place. Although I didn't know it at the time, the day that I made this figure, I actually conceived.

Working in clay I connected to the healing mother archetype residing in my interior world, which was waiting there to help me become a mother myself. Support from my analyst and people on the outside wasn't enough. Through artwork, the forces within me could help me receive and develop the images that my ego could accept and integrate. In order to create new life I had to wrestle with my fears of death by making something tangible, solid and real. The medium of clay allowed me to bring the archetypal energies to consciousness and, by so doing, shape my own earth. Then the mother image could be reborn, and I could become a mother.

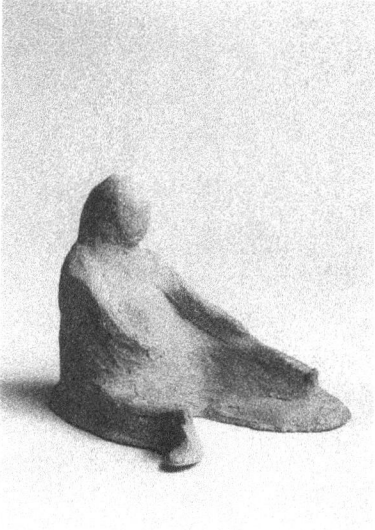

Fig. 9: *My hand on my knee.*

Fig. 10: *The Self holding my ego.*

Figs. 11–12: *The couples.*

Fig. 13: *The birth.*

Fig. 14: *Mother and child.*

Fig. 15: *Standing figure.*

Seven years into our marriage I gave birth to our son. It was a wonderful birth, but it did not entirely escape the threat of death. Three weeks before our son was born, my husband had a ruptured appendix with peritonitis, and he almost died. Not only did this threaten a repeat of a parent's death, but there was another echo from the past. At the time of my own birth my father was in the hospital with perforated ulcers. Fate had our newborn son experience a near-repeat of my own beginnings. After our son's birth, my husband had to return to the hospital, and six days after the birth, he underwent a second surgery. We clung to life during his precarious and rocky recovery. This was a particularly crucial moment of transcendence for all three of us, and we all made it through.

After the birth of our son I made one additional figure of a nursing mother emerging from the head of a dark, earthy figure (fig. 16A–B). The mother, baby and the chthonic ("pertaining to the gods and spirits of the underworld"[30]) figure are in the center of a lotus. In Egypt the lotus symbolizes "nascent life" or "first appearance." In Hindu mythology the eight-petaled lotus is the Heart of Being where the Brahma is.[31]

Fig. 16A–B: *Nursing mother.*

With the new beginning before me, and a near-death behind me, a scar emerged on my breast. This scar was in the form of a star, and I later connected it to the star that completed the last of the series of paintings on the keloid. This was an amazing occurrence, for it was the first time a scar had appeared in a recognizable shape and the first glimmer I had that the scars might have a meaning far beyond what I had fathomed. When this scar arose spontaneously like the others, I had an entirely different reaction to it. I knew the scar had come to mark an event and make it memorable, but this scar had a benevolent feel, as if something inside me was acknowledging and reflecting my achievement and growth. It was bringing a blessing and expressing it in the form of the scar. I sensed that this something was alive inside me, wanting my attention and creating these keloids to make its presence known.

As my analytic work progressed, my star continued to shine. In my outer life the next significant stepping stone in my professional carrier was being accepted into training to become a Jungian analyst. This was a long cherished dream that had seemed out of reach. It was now going to become a reality. I was in my mid-thirties, the mother of a healthy growing boy, and I was studying the work of Jung. During the seven years I was in the training program I had to return repeatedly to the unconscious to reckon with ever-deeper meanings behind my orphan complexes to gain more clarity and insight about them. This diminished their negative effects on me and on my relationships. The scars held me to it. In the past, I had projected the lower side of the psyche on the keloid. Now something was changing. Through the dream of the flowers, the artwork and the scar forming a star, the keloid was beginning to reveal its higher form, a connection to the positive spirit awakening in me. I was beginning to tap into a deeper layer of the scars' reality.

To keep that essence alive, the keloids had to remain. They were an integral part of the equation. The scars seemed to know it, so to speak, and thus the surgery in my childhood hadn't been able to eradicate them. When I tried to remove the already established scars in the group healing ceremony during college, the most valuable ingredient of my life was threatened with extinction. I was like Georgiana in Nathaniel Hawthorne's story "The Birth-mark." Her facial mark was intricately connected with her heart and "clutched its grasp into [her] being."[32] Her husband tried to remove her visible mark of earthly imperfection that was a reflection of mortality, and she died.

What I didn't understand when I wanted the scars removed was that the scars were playing a role in containing the part of my psyche that was out of control. The scars' appearance had caused me added suffering, but they also ensured that I feel the pain I was experiencing and not repress it. Experiencing it in all its depth would ensure that in the future I might integrate this pain into my psychological life.

The potential for darkness to accompany new birth was basic to my myth. Four years after the birth of our son, when I reached thirty-five, the age my mother had been when she died, I was diagnosed with cervical carcinoma in situ. I had cryosurgery with no complications, and the condition did not return, but the synchronicity alarmed me. There was another aspect of the anniversary syndrome at play: my mother died twelve years after my parents' marriage, and the disease erupted twelve years into my own marriage. This time around, just days before the anniversary, a counterbalance to the pull of death appeared on the scene.

A man came along who looked quite like my father, and I was captivated. Psychologically I was still living in the shadows of my father's psyche, and this man embodied many aspects of my father's unlived life and of my own newly-developing creative side. It was too overwhelming to resist, and we began an affair. As this was happening, my husband was invited to teach for a year in another town, providing a temporary separation that solved the problem in the short term. Throughout these early years of our marriage I had been struggling to keep afloat within the vagaries of the psyche's fluctuations. Becoming a mother had taken precedence over my relationship with my husband. The combination left room for a third person to enter, bringing in a spirit that had to surface in a tangible way.

Through the intensity of this new relationship I was able to make significant strides in my creative life and become more conscious of my feminine aspects. I don't think this could have occurred in any other way. Looking at the deeper levels of the affair an astonishing realization came to me. The man was an artist like the protagonist in *Gods' Man*, the book of woodcuts my father had "read" to me. In the book, the artist's model/prostitute revealed her true nature when she showed him the dollar sign on her shoulder. I made the connection to the keloids on my shoulder and how I had been identified with my father's anima,[33] infiltrating my own "prostitute" shadow side. In the book the prostitute betrays her lover unmercifully, and I saw that, though to a lesser degree, I was capable of a similar offense. In part I was expressing my rage at my early struggles and wanting other people to pay for them and relive them with me.

Painful as it was for my husband and son, the affair was nevertheless an important initiation for me. As we all worked through it, it became an important initiation for them as well. Yet because of the pain involved, it will always remain an open question for me whether it had to be done this way. Fortunately, I had a dream at the time that my wedding ring was dented but not broken. In large part because this dream helped me realize that our marriage was still intact, we managed to come back together and slowly mend. Our son weathered the damage to his secure environment, but it no doubt left an imprint on his emotional life.

The transformative impact of this whole event came in a dream. Another layer of the keloid was about to unfold.

> *My close male friend, whose relationship to me was very healing, was eating my scars, and they were grapes.*

My artist friend was eating my scars and digesting what they represented. He had encouraged my creativity and had offered me a strong hand to keep me in life — a counter to death's hand that my mother had to take. As an inner figure, he was participating in a transformation and rebirth mystery. Eating the scars as grapes means integrating them so their meaning can be assimilated. Grapes are a connection to Dionysus, and in the affair I had fallen into the cult of Dionysus and his mysteries. The Dionysian cult was related to fertility and regeneration, both physical and spiritual. In its uncontrolled growth, the keloid scar tissue is like a Dionysian orgy. Creative work changed the unbridled aspect of the keloid scars and turned them into grapes, just as standing on the side of new birth and overcoming my fear of new life had contributed to forming the scar in the shape of a star. In a similar way, the keloids turned into flowers following the prayer ceremony.

In *The Mythic Image*, Joseph Campbell includes a picture of "Dionysus as the Deified Grape," indicating the grape's transformation aspect, "the immanent divinity that had been there in the grape all along"[34] (fig. 17). Within the keloid, the "immanent divinity" would eventually be revealed.

Fig. 17: *Dionysos-Botrys, The Deified Grape. Reprinted from*
The Mythic Image, *by Joseph Campbell: Princeton, Princeton*
*University Press, 1974, fig. 221 (illustration from a first-century*
*A.D. Roman fresco, found in Pompeii, "Bacchus and Vesuvius,"*
*in the collection of Museo Archeologico Nazionale, Naples, Italy)*
*by permission of Scala/Art Resource, NY.*

CHAPTER FOUR

# THE FAMILY FIRE

*All the libido that was tied up in family bonds must be*
*withdrawn from the narrower circle into the larger one, because*
*the psychic health of the adult individual, who in childhood was a*
*mere particle revolving in a rotary system, demands that*
*he should himself become the centre of a new system.*[35]

When Jung talked about the layers of the skin as protection against
outside influences while harboring the divine within, he could have
been talking about the keloid. He wrote: "The same motif is expressed
by the petals of the lotus and by the skins of the onion: the outer layers
are withered and desiccated, but they protect the softer inner layers."[36]

For the divine aspect of the scars to be made conscious, more aspects
of my orphan psychology had to be resolved. My mother's death had
compromised my connection to the divine spirit, but the spirit itself was
not extinguished. On the contrary, this force that wanted to be lived
was using my body to bring itself to birth. As pieces of the Self incarnated in matter, they arose from adversity and became keloid scars.

The search for the origins of my scars equaled and eventually
became integral to the search for my mother. I thought that if I could
"bring her back," I could bring back my innocence and clear myself of
the crime I thought I had committed: that my birth had brought about
my mother's death. I was afraid that my scars substantiated my identity as a criminal. Like the witches on trial in Salem, who when found
to have scars, birthmarks, or deformities were accused and hanged, I
felt that my body was tainted with death and that the scars were the
"the smoking gun," further proof of my guilt. A dream helped to bring
this belief to consciousness.

*I am in a public rest room. I open the stall door and witness a murder.*
*The blood flows onto me. Next I am standing outside, and the wind is blowing*
*shards of glass, and the shards stick to my skin. I overhear the two killers*
*talking about setting me up to take the blame. I know I have to testify to save*
*my life.*

The murder in the dream took place in a public forum, attesting to the collective level of the drama that I was living. Work on this dream revealed that there were collective issues at play. I was taken back to 1939, the year I was born and World War II began. An outbreak of destructive powers was in motion worldwide. Millions of people ultimately suffered and died. In my own life I was experiencing a fragment of this sizable piece of collective shadow as it was flying everywhere. Death, tragedy, and suffering were alive in the collective psyche, and at a deep level no one was spared. This also describes my individual experience of darkness and the pervasive impact it had on me. The gods had broken out of their container, and I could not escape the darkness that had been unleashed.

While working on this dream, a corresponding event came to my attention. After the atomic bomb was dropped on Hiroshima, some survivors of the radiation developed keloids as a result of their burns. The survivors, it is reported, felt guilt, shame, and self-condemnation in the face of the others' deaths. Their keloids were visible reminders of the horror they had experienced, and they considered them marks of disgrace (fig. 18). Despite the enormity of difference between their experience and mine, the feelings these victims (the

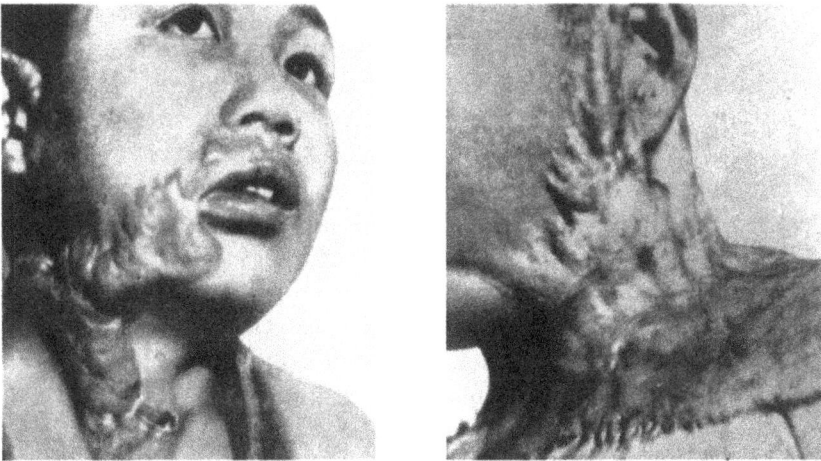

Fig. 18: *Sufferers burnt by heat-rays. Reprinted from Hiroshima brochure by The Japan Council of A and H Victims' Organizations, July, 1965.*

*hibakusha*) expressed were similar to my own. Robert Lifton, in *Death in Life*, interviewed one of them.

> I have a special feeling that I am different from ordi-
> nary people . . . that I have the marks of wounds — as
> if I were a cripple . . . that I am inferior to them . . . of
> course physically, but also mentally . . . . Ordinary
> people don't have this kind of scar. They don't have
> to experience the feeling of humiliation that I have
> had . . . . I imagine a person who has an arm or a leg
> missing might feel the same way . . . . It is not a matter
> of lacking something . . . but rather . . . a handicap —
> something mental which does not show . . . the feeling
> that I am mentally different . . . and incompatible
> with ordinary people . . . .[37]

Lifton went on to write:

> [T]he stigmata assume affirmative significance — on
> the order of what Saint Paul called 'marks of the Lord
> Jesus on my body.' But more often these ennobling
> associations are weak or absent. The keloid then
> comes closer to the pre-Christian meaning of the stig-
> ma as a mark or brand for slaves and criminals, and
> to the related 'post-Christian' idea . . . : 'A mark of
> disgrace or infamy.' Most of all, it takes on the recent
> medically influenced meaning . . . an 'indication of
> disease' — in which the 'disease' mars not only the
> bodily surface but the entire idea of the self.[38]

The collective level of the psyche played a role in my feelings of guilt and my experience of blame. Deeper analytic work would have to be done before the guilt would release its grip on the core of my being. Jung's words brought this guilt into a totally new perspective and pointed the way to a resolution.

> [T]he first step in individuation is a tragic *guilt*. The
> accumulation of guilt demands *expiation* . . . .
> Individuation cuts one off from personal conformity

and hence from collectivity. That is the guilt which the
individual leaves behind him for the world, that is the
guilt he must endeavor to redeem. He must offer a ransom in place of himself, that is, he must bring forth
values which are an equivalent substitute for his
absence in the collective personal sphere.[39]

Latent in the dream was an indication that my testimony would be my
ransom and could redeem the effects of my mother's death. Testifying
would also be avenging her death. My blood, and the libido it would
take to make such a testimony, would bring renewal. I would be able
to better integrate the effects of the collective guilt that comes to each
person who tries to live more consciously. On the personal level, the
killer was also in me. By being too tentative and fearful, I was indeed
guilty of not speaking up for others, of not facing down the dark
forces. Rather, I silently joined the destructive energies, killing the
spontaneous energy that would have me more fully engage in life.
I could no longer use my early fate as an excuse to hide and to stay
safe. Now I was accountable.

My need for outside acceptance had its roots in my hope that I
would be found innocent of the crime of my mother's death. There is
a Gnostic saying that one can't be redeemed for a sin one hasn't committed. Ultimately I would have to integrate this fundamental truth.
The shards of glass[40] in the dream brought to mind an image in the
Kabbalah (Jewish mystical writing) of Isaac Luria (1534–1572) of the
breaking of the vessels: "the primal light . . . was poured into vessels,
but the vessels broke and the light spilled out into the darkness and
now has to be collected again."[41] In trying to become more conscious
I attempted to collect that light. By testifying to the objective truths
and my subjective feelings about them, I could create an entirely new
vessel from which I could live.

Further writing on this important dream brought up my father's
involvement. Blame flew all about in the family house like the glass
shards sticking to my skin. What was unspoken between my father
and me was our common sin and underlying guilt. My father wor-
shipped his queen, his lost wife, and I did too. My stepmother carried
the dark side of the feminine for him, and he projected the positive
side on my mother. She carried his soul for him. Basically, he longed
for his own soul, but he was separated from it because he projected it

outside. I was caught up in this loss, and it became my search for his soul. We clung to each other while suffering these merging energies. In an oedipal embrace, I wanted to redeem my father's tragic life.

As far back as I can remember I wanted to live within my father's inner drama. I had an overwhelming need to live for him, to reflect his moods and feelings, and to find myself in him. As a child I was in love with my father, and in my adult world I was still in love with him. I felt he was longing for the mistress, death, and I joined him in this longing. Love and death began to merge in my psyche at this point, which led to a sacrificial stance. Psychologically, I continued to live in the shadows of his psyche. It was my way of staying warmly tied to him. In the early years it gave me the sense of security I desperately needed. In later years, it was a way to not experience my aloneness.

While my inner life as a child was totally preoccupied with fantasies and longings for my mother, my outer life was taken up with my love for and dedication to my father. Integral to my incestuous connection to him was my attempt to recapture a piece of my mother that he carried by his association with her. I could absorb some of her essence through his embrace. Having only one living natural parent intensifies the attachment to that parent. I cherished the moments I had with my father before the return of the dark and jealous step-mother interrupted them.

The extent to which I was affected by my father's psychology and how much it determined my view of the world was confirmed when, as an adult, I drew a self-portrait. I painted a picture of myself looking into a mirror and saw a reflection of my father looking back (fig. 19). When his face emerged on the canvas I suddenly had an "aha" experience as I realized that I was looking at life through my father's eyes. This explained much of my behavior, my attitudes, and my emotional life, which had never felt completely my own. The shift in my perspective was practically instantaneous once I made this discovery. Work on the father complex had to be undertaken as it was pivotal to my further integration. I couldn't develop my own personality unless I dealt with my identification with my father and the illusion of protection I felt with his image wrapped around me. This identification kept me in a state of naiveté and perilous innocence. I wasn't consciously aware of all this until the dream brought it to my attention.

I had clearly identified with and sacrificed myself to my father far beyond what I had imagined. I can best describe this through our mutual connection to *Gods' Man*. Neither the protagonist of the book nor my father could face the discovery of the mercenary anima, and both fled from the insight. A materialistic attitude pervaded my family, and the whore aspect was lived out in my father's fantasy life as revealed by the women (voluptuous movie stars, for example) he admired. These anima aspects went underground into his incestuous connection to me, and I identified with them. Mainly I felt that I should be supported like "the kept woman" who doesn't need to work in the world. I wanted whoever and whatever would stand in for me and carry my weight.

*Gods' Man* was my father's hopeless cry from his experience of being sacrificed to his inner feminine wiles, and I was impregnated with his cry. By indulging the hope of being taken care of and not furthering my own potential, I was betraying my creative nature. I was turning against my own unconscious, leaving it as my mother had left me. The creative soul is always in danger of being overwhelmed by the demand of the work, and the descent into the unconscious that is required to fulfill the creative task filled me with fear. However, powerful feminine figures were beginning to emerge in my dreams. One such figure suggested I explore a Greek myth to further my understanding of the father complex.

*A female deity directs me to read a book on Iphigenia.*

Fig. 19: *My father in the mirror.*

71

In Greek mythology, Iphigenia, the daughter of King Agamemnon, was sacrificed by her father in order to gain favorable winds for the Greek fleet to sail to Troy.[42] This was a myth I had been living. I was the sacrifice to allow my father's anima to survive after my mother's death, and I was being sacrificed to my stepmother to permit my father's life to go on.

Many aspects of this myth were relevant to my own. Sacrifice was a crucial issue I had to consider in its dual aspects. Up to then I felt I was to be an offering to my father in the name of my mother. Being offered up as a sacrifice gave my life a meaning and a purpose. It explained why I stayed on my father's lap psychologically for so many years, long after his death. It was inflating and brought me the illusion of power. In such a state the ego hangs between total annihilation and rebirth. To avoid annihilation, I had to abandon the role of scapegoat for the grief and suffering of others. I had remained entangled in these forces to preserve what parental structure I had. Now I had to decide how I could change my identity as the passive sacrificial object and make not only a conscious sacrifice but also a meaningful one.

Another personal association came up in my reading about this myth. Iphigenia, in her role as high priestess of Artemis, was entitled to receive the clothes of rich women who had died in childbirth.[43] Here was one place where the two sides of the mother came together in my life. The wealthy women's clothes from the rummage sale that my stepmother wanted me to wear, from one perspective, kept me in the poor orphan role. But on the positive side, they expressed my longing to be clothed in the "wealth" of my real mother and the life principle she represented.

A short time later another name from Greek lore came up in a dream, a name I had no conscious memory of having known: Orestes, Iphigenia's brother. Orestes' fate centered around his need to avenge his father's death. Orphaned at ten, Orestes, when he became a man, consulted the Delphic Oracle as to whether or not he should destroy his father's murderers. His mother Clytaemnestra and her lover had murdered his father Agamemnon. Apollo's answer, authorized by Zeus, was that if he neglected to avenge Agamemnon he would become an outcast from society, barred from entering any shrine or temple "and afflicted with a leprosy that ate into his flesh, making it sprout white mold."[44] The theme of avenging the death of my mother became conscious in me after reading this myth and had a parallel in the dream of the murder and the need for me to testify. The spontaneous scars were the equivalent of leprosy. As a teenager, even though I was not very studious, I read everything I could on the subject of leprosy because I felt a deep kinship with the people afflicted with this disabling disease. Now it was taking on a deeper meaning.

In the myth, with Apollo's protection and through a ruse, Orestes managed to kill both Clytaemnestra and her lover. One version has it that his sister Electra met Orestes at Agamemnon's tomb and recognized him as her brother through a scar on his forehead.[45] As more parallels to my own personal myth came forth in this reading, I began to sense a universal theme in the scars. At an unconscious level I had felt I had to avenge my mother's death and take retribution on myself. This led me to impossible demands on myself, and at the same time putting myself down. In needing to avenge her death I became a sacrificial object by keeping myself lower. I was killing my Self and my creative functioning. I was not taking my rightful place.

Beyond the important similarities between this myth and my own, another significant element needs to be noted: that the unconscious would provide specific references to help me become more conscious. The fact that my psyche had even kept Greek names in storage, names which were not in my consciousness, affirmed to me the authenticity of the collective layer in the unconscious. An additional level of sacrifice was being made: the unconscious was sacrificing itself in offering me access to culture, literature, and education, sending me dreams with references that were not in my conscious repertoire. Furthermore, the unconscious was resisting the pull within itself that counters new life and wants to remain unconscious. To cooperate in the emergence of this light, the ego would make a conscious sacrifice to give the unconscious a receptive ear and, after receiving the morsels it sent up, to act upon the wisdom received. These were the forces I experienced while my ego sat at the helm, catching glimpses of the dark and light elements that had gripped my vital energies.

Concentrating on my father brought his appearance in the following dream:

*My father comes to me and apologizes for the suffering of my childhood. It is very touching to me.*

This personal admission of guilt from my father had a decided impact on my psyche. It authenticated my objective existence, helping me to detach further from the family psyche and to stand on my own. With my father's apology I was released from the personal guilt that I had always felt, especially in his presence. With his apology came permission to continue the work on the blame I had taken on and to which I had sacrificed myself. My father's apology also helped release a lot of anger that was buried in the issue of blame. The dream of the murder had indicated that this anger had to be fully acknowledged. In the midst of working on my father's involvement in this, I found myself shouting, "You participated in making her pregnant. I have paid for your sins. The blood is on your hands now, not mine."

Expressing my anger "openly" meant that I allowed into consciousness something I hadn't wanted to admit. It was as if I had been carrying his sins and trying to redeem them. My life and his were wrapped around my mother's death and would continue to be, until everyone in my inner life and everyone on whom I projected my inner figures was satisfied that the debt had been paid. His apology in the dream and my receiving and accepting it paid that debt. If I could now live for myself and my own values and insights, I would be releasing him to go on his way.

As I absorbed the deeper levels of meaning in this dream I began to consider the positive and redeeming essence that was born from my relationship with my father. For one thing, the artist that was inherently in me was awakened by our reading *Gods' Man.* Equally significant was the fact that I owed my professional career to my father's encouragement to be independent and to take care of myself. As I was trying to assume more responsibility for my life, his apology freed something in me and helped my professional identity solidify.

Another resolution was emerging in regard to the second-place position I had always felt, not only in relationship to my mother, but also in relation to my next older sister. A dream I had as an adult brought up a memory I had repressed.

> *I am walking down the street with Jung, and in the dream*
> *I realize we are at the place where, in my literal childhood,*
> *my father had said to me about my sister:*
> *"She looks just like your mother" and I had been crushed.*

When I was a teenager, I was sitting on the porch with my father, and my sister was walking up the street. The dream picked it up from there. When my father looked longingly at my sister on that day, I was painfully aware that my bond with him was in our identification with one another and that my sister carried the projection of his ideal woman. All my efforts to be his favorite had been in vain. My unconscious had long kept in storage the hurt I felt on that day when he said sadly, "She looks just like your mother." This was now being resolved by my living connection to Jung and the psyche, replacing the anima I had wanted to be.

Dreams about Jung were always deeply meaningful for me. He came bearing wisdom, clarifying the significant psychological issues in my life that needed healing, and this dream was no exception. I began to view my orphan drama from a different angle. I was thrown out of paradise with my mother's death and was then held by my father. Connecting to him was like being held by the Divine, for, at depth, the love of God is behind the father/daughter relationship. Then, Jung became a father figure for me, and correspondingly, he carried the divine spirit I ultimately sought and that resided in my transference to him. Finally I began to make an individual connection to the Divine, separate from the father, and to help that along I needed to retrieve this memory of my initial crushed feelings, so they could resurrect in a way that would be genuinely my own.

Another dream continued this theme and offered a way of releasing the bond that had been intricately woven between this sister and my mother in my own psyche.

*My sister asks a woman to model two dresses that belonged to our mother. My sister has kept our mother's clothes and books in a closet, and she has the key to the closet in her purse. She is now handing it over to me. My stepmother is watching this transaction from a darkened background.*

My sister had carried the idealized Self for me, and I looked up to her with adoration. I felt inferior to all that she was and did. My sister complex had been holding the key to a genuine connection to the Self and to the nourishing mother. A reconnection to the mother image and to her clothes was a reconnection to the ancestry of my womanhood. This could allow more of my own feminine qualities to emerge. The key was now in my possession.

At the same time that this momentous shift was taking place, the dark mother's presence surrounded the event with a miasmic cloak. Inevitably she stands at the gate of new life, this time at the "passing of the guard." She doesn't want me to have the key. In my journal during this time I wrote: "She watches me, jealous of the creative dance. She waits for the music to stop, and she pulls me out of the room, my hand in her hand, and she bursts out: 'I'll show you — you think you're so smart!' Her poison gets into me. I am imbued with it. I become jealous like her." The urge for transformation and for the eternal is inevitably opposed by demons. It was hard to get out from under this gaze, the gaze of the objector-to-life.

The dark mother image inevitably appears inside the wound of the motherless child, the polar opposite to the fantasy of the good mother. The real mother carries the ancestor-spirit, and the stepmother carries the chthonic feminine. The negative mother pulls one back into the mire of undifferentiated unconsciousness. The good mother propels one forward into new life. Often for the orphan, darkness comes again to grab the new baby in the form of a negative mother. It is not so much the early death of the parent but the quality of the parent replacement that is a crucial factor in one's future development.

This penetrating force of darkness at the gate of new life also arose from the instinctual layer of the psyche where the image of the animal appears. I would have to experience the feelings I had avoided and create the conditions for a substantial change in my psychology. This layer was displayed in another dream I had about my sister.

> *In front of the house where my sister and I live is a tiger.*
> *I have to walk outside to get to the other side of the house.*
> *The tiger pounces on me, and I think I am going to die.*
> *But then I have the thought: God is between me and the tiger,*
> *and I picture God as a granite slab over me.*
> *The tiger gets up and walks away.*

In order for me to assimilate the positive side of myself (the other side of my psychological house) that my sister initially represented, I had to encounter the tiger. Symbolically, tigers can represent the dark and cruel side of the feminine that I met on the outside — my mother's death, my stepmother and, to a lesser degree, the way my sister and I enacted the orphan drama in our childhood. The tiger represented the anger I had repressed that could devour me if I didn't resolve it. The tiger also represented my envy of this sister who "had what I didn't have." The tiger is the untamed instinctual state of the unconscious, the *nigredo* (the dark, initial state of the alchemical process), the chaos that reflects states of affective nature (envy and self-abnegation). I would have to integrate these states in order to establish their spiritual counterpart. One solution to the envy was to heed the maxim: one does better not to define oneself by what one doesn't have, but by what one does have.

The tiger is a large feline connected to the independence of the psyche that can't be ruled. It represents autonomous aggression. It can devour anything that is around. That meant I had a devouring aspect inside. It also meant I had a powerful potential, for such a tiger has a fiery nature and enormous energy, but I lacked a kind of brutality that was necessary to defend myself. I had become too sweet. I associated the granite slab with the stone an artist uses to reproduce lithographs. The artwork I was producing was as vital to my process as connecting to the image of God. It took me to deeper levels in myself. When I brought aspects of myself into consciousness they offered me protection against the tiger elements in the unknown. It was as if the *imago dei,* an image of God imprinted on the psyche, would save me from being devoured. To be saved I had to live my life with a spiritual attitude foremost and central to my being. Psychologically it would mean living my life out of a transpersonal purpose that the image of God evoked, and not wanting a purely material existence. I had to keep connecting to my potential wholeness, which included my positive side, and not identify incessantly with my inferior side, as I had done in relation to my sister. This could help me create a more conscious and rational standpoint and objectify not only my relationship with her on the outside but also my relationship with my own more developed side that had been projected onto her.

When I lived closer to the spiritual dimension that was so much a part of my being, I was keeping the psyche in the forefront of my mind. It would help protect me from the devouring aspect of the unconscious and from complexes that threatened to attack me like a tiger. Worshipping my sister was worshipping a false god. This insight held the key. When the tiger complex attacked me, my connection to the Self and my totality was at risk. It could destroy my life potential. When I put myself down, one side of me was devouring the other side. When I was out from under this tiger I could make my way into the world. Correspondingly, getting to the other side of myself, the stronger side, would mean integrating the aggressive instincts (such as speaking out), something I was hesitant to do. This would ensure continued allegiance to both the instinctual side and the spiritual side of my natural state.

My oldest sister came up periodically in my dreams, and each image of her indicated a change was taking place. She represented a part of me that had been excluded from my (psychological) house. Now, more of myself was becoming integrated. This led to my writing more about my two mothers — the one in the spirit world and my "earth" stepmother. I came to realize that splitting them deifies one and demonizes the other. I needed to carry the earth [-mother] connection more consciously while integrating the spirit in myself. Then I could better carry these opposites, be more in the world and less outside it. I also needed to integrate more of the darkness that lives within and without.

Pondering these questions resulted in a change in my inner image of the stepmother. She came up frequently in my dreams. One dream among many now showed her imprisoned on the third floor of our house; from there she had no influence on me. In another dream I had four years after I ended my analysis:

> My stepmother has hired four men to repair the stove in the kitchen where I grew up.

The kitchen was the center of my psychological house, and the stove was the fire burning there. The number four represents wholeness. This repair meant that my total personality would be affected. When I consulted the four men in an active imagination it was revealed that they were connected to and became my grandfather, my father's father, whom I had never met but whom I had admired from hearing about him. His image had never come to me before, and he was one ancestor that I wished I had met. Here was an opportunity to know him, and it was a relationship born from my association with the stepmother forces. Cinderella came to mind. Perhaps she wouldn't have found the prince if she hadn't had the stepmother she did, for it was through Cinderella's despair that the fairy godmother was invoked.

The deep abyss I experienced at my beginning had to be revisited over and over and processed slowly so that the darkness and the light that accompanies it could gradually become integrated. The unconscious had used the symbol of blood to describe the dramatic circumstance of my birth and its aftermath. Now it used the symbol of fire. Both gave evidence that my psyche and my body had been scarred, and slowly a healing was taking place, as was shown in this dream about fire.

*Years ago a family had been in a fire.*
*Now, in the present time, the baby of the family*
*is being wheeled along in a carriage,*
*enveloped in a cocoon of healing skin.*
*She was the family member most affected by the fire.*
*The father, too, had burns all over his body;*
*walking behind them is the mother, who also*
*had been badly burned.*
*The older sister was slightly burned in two places,*
*but they all had suffered and they all are healing.*

It was clear from this dream that not only me but all the members of my family had been affected by my mother's death. The dream also referred to the many facets of my own psychology that had been affected; these facets were reflected in the family members. Nevertheless each member of my family had in fact endured the fire, and, according to the dream, now we all were healing. Even though I wasn't physically with them, during our brief contacts my own changes resulted in a difference in the way we related. To the extent I could become conscious of old family patterns, I was less likely to pass along the disagreeable features to future generations.

# CHAPTER FIVE

# UNCOVERING THE JEWEL

*Illnesses, like these keloids, in spite of their destructive aspect,*
*are like the dancing Shiva who has the club and the sword and the*
*drum in his many hands, but has one hand out in front raised in the*
*gesture that says: Fear not. This illness is peculiarly yours, and if you*
*follow where it leads . . . it will bring you to those who are your own*
*kin, and to your own particular experience of your destiny which*
*reaches, in this way, beyond death.*[46]

Over the course of my analysis, I was training to be an analyst, solidifying my relationship with my husband, working as a psychotherapist, and raising our son. During this time, a few new scars appeared on my back. Because they could be easily covered up and were not in my line of vision they didn't bother me as much. I was hard at work on my inner life, and that was absorbing all my attention. The scars themselves, however, did not want to be ignored. They itched quite a lot to keep me attentive to their presence. I had grown to accept the troublesome nature of this pruritis, but my analyst encouraged me to see if there were any new medical procedures that could remedy this aspect of the keloid condition.

In the late 1960's when my husband and I were in Zurich, I went to a medical clinic for a consultation about the scars. The doctor there tried a new approach — Novocain injections directly into the scars on my chest — to no avail. Several years later in Los Angeles I tried corticosteroid injections on the same scars, but they remained unchanged. It seemed the scars had been present too long for these treatments to be effective.

I consulted a physician who, during the examination, lanced an acne lesion on my back that had the potential for becoming a scar. This triggered another iatrogenically induced keloid. Following this unexpected development, the doctor invited me to be one of several patients present at an annual convention of dermatologists, who gathered together to study difficult cases. I sat on the examining table, and as the doctors paraded through, they asked a recurring question: "Did anything happen to cause these scars?" I offered my psychological theory, but they would have none of it. I felt humiliated and exposed. When the doctors gathered later for their general discussion, they didn't come up with a solution for preventing or removing the scars, but years later I had another experience in a medical setting that turned out to be an antidote to this scene.

I was inspired to do some research of my own that would involve interviewing people with keloids. To access the patient population, I made an appointment with a dermatologist who had been receptive to me when I broached the idea. As I sat in the waiting room before our appointment I began to lose focus on why I was there, and for a few minutes, I thought I was a patient coming to consult the doctor. The emotions that position often evokes began to rise. I felt some anxiety, and I felt small in relation to the doctor, who carried the authority. Fortunately a subsequent thought turned the whole thing around. I realized: "This interview is about the psyche. I know more about this element of the scars' evolution than he does." With that thought I regained my professional persona and an appropriate relationship to the situation.

The Self was behind me, and our meeting went well, but he said he could support my research only if my questions related solely to how people felt about their scars. He said he couldn't endorse the line of inquiry that explored the cause as potentially psychological — much less archetypal. I didn't follow through with that research project, but through dreams and artwork I was beginning to find more evidence of the psyche's involvement in keloid scar formation, and I hoped someday to reclaim the keloid's rightful place among psychogenically induced dermatological problems. By clearing its name, I could clear my own.

The experience in the waiting room was the significant moment I needed, because it helped me see that anything to do with the scars inevitably lured me into feeling inferior. Without a moment's notice I had identified with the less differentiated side of the psyche. It took concentrated reflection for me to remember that the scars carried two sides: on the one hand, the insult of disfigurement and the wound they both caused and reflected and, on the other, an offer of healing and protection. Beneath these opposites the deepest most dramatic layer of the scar was about to be revealed. What I was about to discover would give my life direction, purpose, and a meaning far beyond anything I could have anticipated.

I happened one day to leaf casually through a book on Mesopotamian art[47] that we had on our bookshelf. I came upon some photographs of a male figurine adorned with pellets of clay on his torso in the same places where the scars on my chest, arms and shoulder had developed (fig. 20). I was spellbound by what I saw. I immediately turned to the text to find out more about them, but it didn't specifically explain the significance of the pellets of clay. So I explored further and found that they represented scarification — that is, intentional scarring.

Anthropologists thought the little figures were placed in graves to provide comfort and dignity to the deceased in the next world. Scholars have been unable to determine the exact significance of these artifacts, but because they were associated with the dead and presented features emblematic of the gods of the underworld, they are viewed as chthonic deities. They were also thought to symbolize fertility and life, because the figurines were placed on the pelvis of the dead. The keloid myth was unfolding before my eyes.

The meanings associated with these ancient artifacts were the orphan opposites I was living with: the pull toward and fascination with my mother's death and my longing for rebirth, fertility, and life. This was the first time I felt an authentic connection between the keloids and my mother in her grave. Intuitively I knew the scars had carried my long-standing psychological attitude in regard to my mother, but there had been no concrete evidence to validate this supposition. Now, not only were the metaphysical roots of the keloid scars being shown to me, but the archetype of the scar was merging with the archetype of the orphan.

When I saw the historical origins of the keloid archetype, the jewel began to show itself. This archetypal dynamic held the potential for a complete transformation of my life. Investigating the rites of scarification would be a way to explore this, but since it would need some reflection, I put that aside for later. The keloid was a microcosm of my psychology, and that meant I would have to reach the deepest layers of my psyche to comprehend fully the beginnings of the keloid's evolution that these photographs revealed. As I came to understand it, this required reliving the chaos in my depths more concretely than I had done before. I would have to descend into the chaos, as it were, to extract the jewel that was buried there.

Fig. 20: *Mesopotamian figurine with pellets of clay on his torso. Reprinted from* The Art of Mesopotamia *by Eva Strommenger and Max Hirmer: London, Thames and Hudson, 1964, fig. 12 (Terracotta male figurine from Eridu, side and front views, early Warka period, first half of the 4th millennium B.C., Iraq Museum, Baghdad), by permission of Hirmer Verlag (München) GmbH and the Iraq Museum, Baghdad, Republic of Iraq.*

For me the jewel was discovering more about the meaning of my scars and, secondly, resolving the longing for and identification with my mother. Meditating on the figurine revealed my underlying wish to be with my mother in her grave. The scars, by keeping my focus on them, had kept me from becoming conscious of this depression. They protected me by expressing what I could not express consciously. Yet I would need another somatic expression of the depression to become more acquainted with the chaos of which it was made.

On the outside I was managing very well, but inside I was still the Little Match Girl, standing outside my life looking through the window at what others had. The flame of my match illuminated the nourishment given to others that I felt I was missing. Now, the longed-for hearth fire burned furiously and lodged in my intestines. From its intense heat I developed ulcerative colitis. This intestinal disease was evidence of my continuing involvement with the dark power that was constellated at my birth. Then, the earth that I had entered suddenly lost its foundation. Now it was happening again.

The most common symptoms of ulcerative colitis include bloody diarrhea, abdominal pain, weight loss, and anemia. Because the colon has more nerve endings than any other organ in the body, it is particularly susceptible to psychological influences. Fear is associated with peristalsis; gastric mucosa pales with fear. The colon is subject to every mood. Fear had been pervasive from my earliest days, and now my colon was expressing it. When I ruminated on the colitis I noted repeated and converging psychological factors. The precipitating one was my pervasive feeling of abandonment. It seemed intractable. A word, a gesture or a thought would reactivate the early pain and fear that evolved from the loss of the mother, the longing for her return and the hope to find her that I maintained. The blood and liquid feces spoke to the avalanche of grief and unconscious rage at the loss of my mother that I was unable to express consciously. My ulcerated colon was a somatic expression of my psyche's unspoken experience. This was the living chaos that was asking for my attention.

This illness occurred as our son was approaching adolescence. He was becoming his own person and didn't need my close attention. It was time for me to engage in my own creative endeavors rather than standing in the shadow of others, but I was paralyzed by the prospect. I wasn't conscious of how strong the death pull was. The scars could protect me only up to a point. The inner life spoke through the body once more, and I had to listen. In the early months of my illness when I was desperate to get well, I turned again to painting. It would allow the psyche to speak directly to my despairing ego. It was a form of prayer, and I had to give in to it totally. I put up my canvas and got out my paints.

As I stood before the blank canvas I knew I had to go inside myself and express what was there. I gave it everything I had. I was astonished at what appeared. The colors and shapes became a portrait of my mother. In the painting she looked like a Native American, which would become significant later (fig. 21). I was not conscious of calling to her for help, but the psyche had done it for me. That my mother had come across to me on the canvas, unbidden and unexpected, shifted my feelings of being abandoned and alone to a sense of containment in her presence. I had not anticipated that. I had thought she was far away, and I had been forgotten. With the realization that was not the case, my whole body began to relax.

The ulcerative colitis was expressing the deepest layer of my wound, and it was at this level of the psyche that the image of my mother

Fig. 21: *Painting of my mother*

could come into being. Healing did not come overnight, but I am convinced that her presence as an internalized image initiated the process. The unconscious sent me a dream a few months after I did this painting that related to this level of the psyche, suggesting that I had to reach the ancestral stage of the unconscious to effect a significant amount of healing for my colon.

> I was in a hospital, and my cure was to reach into a bucket,
> take out the goldfish and eat them whole.

Eating the fish of gold was the prescribed remedy. One of my first associations to the image of goldfish was to *Wee Fishie Wun*. I had identified with his difficult beginnings and the challenging journey the little fish had to make to become his true self. In my life's journey, this disease and its healing were my current challenge. The emergence of the fish image when I was sick was my psyche's way of connecting me to the deepest layers of the unconscious.

In dreams, the fish as symbol has a double nature. Since Christ is equated with the fish, the fish is a symbol of the Self, a redeeming, saving entity.[48] The fish is venerated as a symbol of the soul, but it is also seen as unclean and represents voraciousness. Fish can represent cold-blooded contents of the psyche that live below the surface of consciousness. I had to assimilate these opposites within my psyche: my highest aspects and my lowest, my early wound and the potential for its transformation. Eating the fish whole meant that I had to accept my totality: the difficult circumstances of my birth and the aftermath, my vulnerabilities and weaknesses, as well as my strengths and abilities. In working on the dream, I realized that the fish in the bucket also represented the creative healing fantasies of the unconscious. To eat them, one by one, would integrate and assimilate the creative forces.

Another dream I had during my illness brought up the dark side of the fish symbol and provided insight into the psychic chaos that had contributed to the creation of the scars and now to the intestinal disease.

> My stepmother sent me a fish in the mail.
> It is so demonic that it is killing all the other fish in the bowl.
> I have to put it in a container by itself.

The destructive aspect of the mother, as seen in this fish, was a potent reminder of the darkness of my childhood. With the coming of the stepmother, the dark side of the fish entered and ate all the other fish. In order to attain insight into its ongoing manifestation indicated in this dream, I did an active imagination[49] with my analyst in the hour following the dream. I took the part of the demon fish, and my analyst asked me (as the fish) why I was so angry. Out of my mouth came: "Because I was blamed for something I didn't do!" I did not say it as an intellectual construct. I felt it to be absolutely true. My analyst responded with an important insight: "One develops the identity of a criminal from such a psychological condition."

The demon fish represented the rage I felt at being blamed for my mother's death. That rage had never reached consciousness, but it was very much alive in my psyche. The rage and guilt I felt, consciously and unconsciously, stood in the way of my creative endeavors. It needed to be isolated until, in its voracious frenzy, it revealed its true nature and I could see how and when it operated. The demon fish dream helped me to isolate the complex, to "put it into a container by itself," as the dream put it, and to endure its transformation. The demon fish living inside me was destroying my sense of myself. It was furiously eating up everything in sight, contaminating my psyche, and at the physiological level, my intestines. Unexamined, its threat was unceasing. Working with the symbol of the fish brought to the surface the dark and light elements that had affected the cells of my colon.

The ulcers gradually healed, and I went on with my life. But the healing didn't last. Something more was required, for a year later I had a relapse. Fortuitously, around this time I was invited to give a lecture. This was the first invitation I had ever received to give a public talk, and it required that I write down my thoughts on paper. I chose the topic of the archetype of the orphan. Expressing myself creatively in writing as I had done with painting and clay had a positive effect on the colon. In consolidating my thoughts through writing on the subject of orphan psychology, I was also regulating my digestive process.

Just as important as writing and identifying psychological issues was my need to produce something tangible, to give material expression to the healing I hoped would take place. To that end, I made a golden image of my intestines in clay (fig. 22). I wanted to show the colon what I hoped it could become. I painted it gold in thanksgiving for its continuing support. I hoped that by creating this image I was upholding new life. My colon's health seemed directly linked to this symbolic representation. The creative effort and what I was beginning to understand

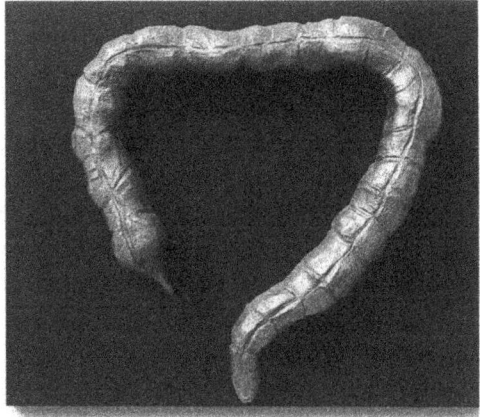

Fig. 22: *Golden image of my intestines in clay.*

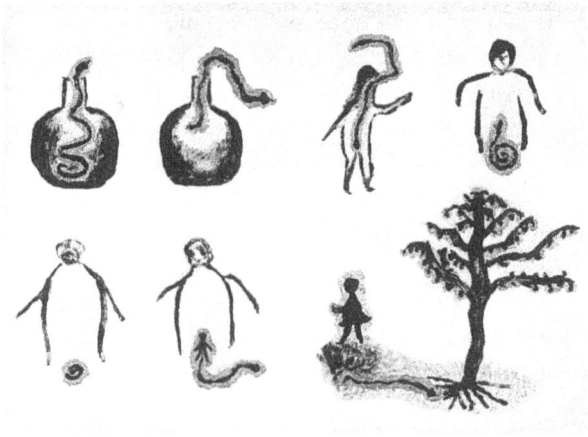

Fig. 23: *My vision of the snake and tree.*

about the myth of the orphan shifted something in my depths so that it could enable me to locate the core issues that surrounded my illness.

The unconscious supported my efforts to heal by once again directing my energy to the inner world for renewal. It sent me a momentous vision. The vision appeared quite spontaneously and was centered around the image of the snake. In its undulating movements and connection with instinct, the snake is symbolically equivalent to the intestines. As the vision unfolded it seemed to express the meaning of my disease in its totality.

> *A snake comes out of a flask and into my mouth.*
> *It goes down into my uterus, incubates there and is born as a snake and child.*
> *The snake impregnates a tree, and fruit hangs from its branches.*
> *The child reaches for the fruit of tree (fig. 23).*

The Self presents itself in dark form first as it comes up from the depths of the unconscious. The psyche had first presented the image of the snake in my childhood dream to represent the chaos. The scars protected me from this chaotic state. Now the snake of my vision once again represented the dark womb of the body and the psyche where the chaos had to be transformed. The snake and tree seemed to have evolved from the early dream in which I was standing before the leafless tree that represented my mother and giving birth to black snakes from my arm. The many snakes had now consolidated into one snake, indicating that a transformation process had taken place in my outer world.

The snake brought with it the needed transformation that would become actualized only far in the future. The snake created the ulcerative colitis, but it also produced the fruit. It expressed the autonomous life force that brought on the disease and, at the same time, provided the wisdom to heal it. Furthermore, the snake's power to renew itself in me could keep alive my link with the eternal element.[50] The scars served the same function.

The vision showed me the task and meaning of my life as it was meant to be lived. Unlike the leafless tree in my childhood dream, the tree in this vision, when fertilized by the snake, bears fruit, the hoped-for rebirth. It was comforting to read that Jung wrote about a patient's dream image of a tree with beautiful fruit: "[T]he first impression is of health, completeness; sickness is overcome."[51] Ingesting the snake was an image of the individuation process incarnating in the body as an illness. When this process is taken up by the work of the ego, it can then express itself in the outer world. This is not an easy task for someone with orphan psychology. Difficulty in accepting adult life and the creative force that accompanies it is a common problem for an orphan. One is tempted to stay in an unborn state, as if wrapped in a protective cloak where everything is safe. But illness signals that a change needs to be made in one's life.

I found solace in Mircea Eliade's remarks about the experience of illness as initiation, its connection to chaos and its redeeming light. He describes the suffering and the solitude inherent in an experience of illness as part of an initiation process that can be viewed as "a symbolic return to Chaos equivalent to preparing a new Creation."[52] Just as the snake in the Garden of Eden resulted in Adam and Eve's loss of innocence, so the appearance of illness means that one will be leaving paradise, voluntarily or involuntarily. To grasp the meaning of one's illness means to lose one's innocence, so eating the snake was like eating the forbidden fruit. For an orphan, the forbidden fruit is life itself and the creativity that belongs to life. Working with the unconscious for the sake of renewal meant defying the dictate of the orphan complex that one must not move forward into new life.[53]

In his seminar on Nietzsche's *Zarathustra*, Jung writes about the snake's connection with the divine and gives an example of eating the snake as initiation.

> The snake is . . . a religious symbol in the mysteries of Sabazios. The initiation consisted in [simulating] the swallowing of the snake . . . . and then [taking it] out below again; it was then assumed that the God had entered the initiant and impregnated him with the divine germ . . . . The serpent symbolizes the god that enters man in order to fill him with the god . . . and the pulling out from below means the birth . . . .[54]

When I read about this initiation ritual a memory came up and took on new meaning. When my son was a small child I had found myself engaging in a ritual with him we both thoroughly enjoyed. We would sit on the floor and pretend he was being born from under my skirt. At the time, I was conscious only of the fact that the pregnancy and his birth had gone so amazingly well and that I wanted to recreate them over and over again. His birth had been a significant initiation for me, as the keloid star had revealed. This passage from Jung helped me see what was underlying our play. At his birth I found new life, not death, and this aspect made the ritual so compelling. It meant that the favorable side of God was alive inside me at my son's birth, and I wanted it to stay.

Two years after my second bout of colitis I had another relapse. This time I rapidly lost weight and energy. It was a sign to me that I had to go even deeper. The only avenue left to me was to go directly to the ulcers themselves in an active imagination and make the descent into their fiery center.

When I reached the interior, to my amazement, my mother was sitting on the edge of the ulcer, and she said to me, *"I will have to die in your life in order that you can live"* (fig. 24A–B ). In that critical moment when my life and my health were at stake, there she was once again, residing in the depths of my body. As had happened with my painting of her, she emerged from the ulcer quite unexpectedly and when I needed her most. Her reaching out from my interior world a second time was indeed a gift from the Beyond.

My mother's message to me was clear. The separation she spoke about seemed like a cruel request now that I had just "found" her. What she conveyed, however, was the urgent imperative that I separate from my identification with her and her early death. If I could achieve that separation, then we could come together in a very different way. In a perpetual state of identification with her, I felt as if my own life and death had already been experienced, and I didn't need to live at all. Her dictate from the colon sent the opposite message: I had to take up my own life. I needed to carry my own experience or I'd burn up from the inside out.

A dream I had about the same time mirrored the active imagination and suggested a way to bring it into life.

> *There in the living room where my mother used to sit by the radiator*
> *is a flattened-out round ossified fish. I think it is dead, but it is not.*
> *Its eye moves around and looks at me. It had been contained in a*
> *buttered wax paper. I put it in a large paper bag already filled with water*
> *that has many other fish in it. There are dark reptilian creatures*
> *trying to get out, but I push them back in. I have to find an*
> *appropriate container for all of them and get the numbers just right.*

Fig. 24A–B: *My mother in the colon.*

Where my mother used to sit was a fish. I thought it was dead, but the eye was moving. The pupil of the eye is where an image of oneself is reflected in the eye of the other,[55] and the fish's eye for me represented the mutual reflection I hoped could happen with my mother and me. The dream indicated she was not dead. Her eyes continued to live. Relating to the unconscious so directly in active imagination and in painting may have contributed to the resurrection of the image of my mother, bringing her alive inside me as indicated in this dream. In addition, it was not only my mother but the autonomous spirit that she represented that had been preserved, and with the work, made more conscious. This ossified fish was like a creative spirit available for my use. Putting it in the water where all my aspects, both dark and light, resided was the continuing work with the unconscious that brought renewal, life, and well-being. A beautiful amplification of this dream appears in Jung's *Alchemical Studies*.

> 'There is in the sea a round fish, lacking bones and scales, and it has in itself a fatness, a wonder-working virtue, which if it be cooked on a slow fire until its fatness and moisture have wholly disappeared, and then be thoroughly cleansed, is steeped in sea water until it begins to shine . . . .' This is the description of the transformation process.[56]

In alchemy it is said that the spirit is hidden in the water like this mythological round fish. It was also known to contain the precious dragon's stone that "becomes a gem only when a bit of the dragon's soul remains inside."[57] Ulcerative colitis was like a dragon. Inside the disease itself was an image of my mother like the jewel that must be retrieved from the dragon when the dragon is still alive so it won't take back the jewel into death.[58] My mother had to be found by revisiting the living wound itself. In the chaos, in the lower and in the dark aspects, life can be renewed.

It took three bouts of colitis over a four-year period for me to begin to understand what this disease was trying to convey. The illness was requiring that my orphan psychology be synthesized into my total personality. To that end, many of the images in my previous dreams came together over this period: ingesting the snake and eating the fruit were reminiscent of the dream of eating the scars as grapes. A living connection to the eternal would need to be a vital ingredient in my psycho-logical diet. This intestinal disease was the tiger I had to encounter to get to the other side of myself. The tower dream had taught me that painting was a way to do it. The psychological and physical healing that came about during and after my inner work testified to its bene-fits. Relating to the unconscious would show that the trauma of the wound and the effects of the blame could be transformed.

The blood in the colon was reminiscent of the murder dream in which I needed to testify and could not play the role of scapegoat, taking the blame and carrying the guilt that belonged to someone else. My father had released me from the blame, and I had the key to my mother's belongings, but the dark mother was standing at the door, the darkness attending the renewal. The dream of my family having endured the fire alluded to the early trauma, but the inner fire that had been set in motion had not died out. The destructive fires were at play in the coli-tis. The dark mother was still present, and I was to experience her in the body. Although I had been given a bigger key, I was paralyzed by the prospect of myself being bigger, surpassing my mother. This illness was both the death pull that seemed so great and the living initiation that was needed.

The ulcerative colitis set the stage for a reunion with my mother, which had to come before I could once again turn my attention to the scars. The experience of illness was as dark and difficult as finding the photographs of the Mesopotamian scarified figurine had been enlightening and compelling. In the figurine I was being shown the next step in my development, and fear of taking this step reverberat-ed throughout my body. My intestines, so acutely sensitive to such feelings, registered my fear of autonomy. The Self wanted to move on, and when my ego hesitated out of fear, the Self presented me with a somatic display of its reaction.

This illness suggested that I needed to sacrifice the passive attitude toward myself and make my whole life creative. The dictate from my unconscious was "create or die." I began to make some outer changes. I eliminated many of my extraverted activities because I felt the need to stay quiet and close to my own process. I moved into a room of my own in our house, carving out a retreat for myself with space for my creative work. I started to take supplements that supported the healing process.

I was fortunate that this illness offered me one final initiation. It gave me a living example of divine intervention that could heal the colon. Only in a profound moment of suffering (similar to my experience of the keloid emerging on my knee) was I able to invoke it. One night before my colon had completely healed, I was trying to go to sleep, and my intestines were highly agitated. It concerned me more intensely than usual. I felt as helpless and distraught as I had when the keloids began to grow out of control. Then I remembered a healing ritual one of my colleagues had suggested: to imagine a beam of light coming through my head and extending down to my intestines. With my whole self I gave in to the light. I concentrated on its descending into me for only a few minutes, and my colon immediately quieted down. I was astounded! Invoking a spiritual attitude in the form of the descending light, as I had done through artwork and active imagination, helped to locate the divine lost in matter.

Colitis was teaching me my own form of divination. It was as if the snake inside me gave an immediate response to the decisions I made. If I took a wrong turn, the snake signaled distress by stirring in my intestines. In its effort to make my conflicts conscious, the colon became the "inner-other" to which I owed allegiance. What I learned from this serious illness was that when the mind and body work together they form the container in which the Self can manifest and the soul can be more consciously realized. Without the full impact of suffering and the experience of grace, body and spirit cannot be reconciled. The process of renewal, born from the unconscious and the body and put into the work, creates an experience of the eternal where one is not alone. To find the eternal is to find an indestructible reason for going on.

# CHAPTER SIX

## MOTHER'S RETURN

*Nothing exerts a stronger psychic effect upon the human
environment, and especially upon children, than the life which
the parents have not lived.*[59]

The "rites of passage" — college, marriage and childbirth — were
not only significant turning points in my outer life but also the cross-
roads of psychological rebirths. Until the colitis occurred I thought it
was only my mother's life that had been worth living and feared that
new growth and development in me would challenge this assumption.

The death of my mother left the door wide open to psychological
and physical chaos. From the depths of my body arose scars that
spoke for me. My fascination with the scars set me on the long road
of integrating the mother loss. The archetype of death at birth and
its connection to the scars was finally beginning to unfold in a way I
could grasp. The search for and integration of the scars' meaning was
accompanied by the need for a living connection to my mother. I
wanted to see her; I yearned for our reunion as Persephone longed to
see her own mother after she was taken down to Hades. I hoped that
my mother, like Demeter, was longing to see me. From the experience
with ulcerative colitis, I had learned the healing value of creative
work. It engaged the deeper layers of the psyche where the image of
my mother resided. Now it wasn't an illness that would bring us
together. A series of dreams gave hints.

> *There are many guests gathered together for an evening of intellectual
> discourse (something I was told my real parents did, but that stopped
> abruptly with the coming of my stepmother).*
> *Outside the house a starved, emaciated lion, weak and dying,
> walks up to the porch and jumps up on a pedestal in order to sit
> "on the highest place."*

Symbolically, lions represent the heat of passion, and my great passion was to experience as much of my mother's essence as was

humanly possible. The lion is also associated with the sun[60] and therefore with consciousness. It is the king of the savanna and often analogous with royalty. What "sits in the highest place" was my highest value, which needed to be lived in all parts of my life — interior and exterior. The house in this dream was the actual residence of a childhood friend who had a cohesive family unit. People often gathered there for lively salons. The starving lion returning to this particular house represented my psyche's highest value, the intellectual culture that I had missed. My mother had been very well read, but life with our stepmother was quite different. Culture, art, and literature had little room in our family. I did not study Greek myths, read Shakespeare, or discuss the classics in my high school or college. In the early years of the training program, I felt inferior to my professional colleagues because of this. The unconscious was insisting that I remedy this situation in my adult life.

Early in my analysis I had a dream that all the trees lining my childhood street were barren. It described my psychological life when I was growing up and may have referred to my psyche's need for more than came to it. Without more intellectual stimulation, the trees surrounding my psychological house would remain barren. In my outer life I was starving from the lack of creative interchange, just as in my emotional life I had been starving for the lack of a mother. This contributed to my strong emotional reaction to being left out of such gatherings in my adult life, whether I imagined the rejection or not.

When I first awoke from this dream of the starving lion I thought of a painting of the *Pietà* I had recently seen, in which Christ was pictured as extremely thin and emaciated. The image reminded me of myself when I was suffering from ulcerative colitis, emaciated and tempting death. I associated this lion with Christ as the sacrifice and with his resurrection. The return of the lion represented the return of my mother when I was sick and in a death-like state. Psychologically, the death and resurrection association meant that I had projected spiritual values on my mother, and that projection had to die. My own connection to these values, independent of her, had to be resurrected. It eventually became apparent that to feed the lion meant I had to feed what was missing in me. Being a sacrifice had taken its toll physically and psychologically.

My ruminations on the question of sacrifice surrounding my birth had preoccupied me and had engaged my consciousness, often taking "the highest place." I had to sacrifice living in the service of my mother to living in the service of the Self and move from a fascination with death toward living life. The focus on my personal mother in my early years was preparation for a more decided connection to the Self in the later ones. At the deepest layer, the lion in the dream represented a powerful aspect of the Self and its resurrection in me. The lion is strong and goes its own way. As an inner lion, it represented the unconscious drive for individuation, and that drive needed to be fed. I concluded that at each subsequent crossroad I encountered, a conscious sacrifice of my identification with my mother had to be made in order to honor her death and my life.

Spurred by the realization that this would create a bridge to the mother, the Self, and to the world of culture buried deep in my own psyche, I began to pursue my creativity and take my urge to write seriously. To that end, the following year I spent a three-week vacation entirely alone to gather my materials and begin to organize my thoughts. This was the first time I had ever stayed alone so long with the specific intent of writing. It turned out to be one of the most productive periods of my life. The following two dreams came at the conclusion of that fruitful incubation. Both referred to the spiritual dynamic within the creative process and its potential for both destruction and salvation.

> *I am dressed in a beautiful white outfit, and my husband is in a black suit.*
> *We are watching a choir of boys singing spiritual songs,*
> *and when my husband shakes the hands of the first two boys in line, he says,*
> *"You know, you are most fortunate to be able to sing these songs.*
> *In earlier times the young boys who were here were stoned for singing."*

On the personal level, being stoned reflected my psyche's view of what had been hurled at me. On the collective level, stoning is associated with punishment and guilt. The guilt and responsibility I had carried for my mother's death were especially relevant here. Carrying blame that does not legitimately belong to the ego destroys it by creating a negative identity, or distorts it by creating an inflation. Either way, one's spirit is compromised in the psychological madness that ensues. Here the madness changed into singing when I could have a moral and ethical attitude toward the unconscious. That meant becoming conscious of collective attitudes and how they had played out in my life. Rather than looking backwards to what I hadn't had,

I needed to see my limitations as an impetus to growth and change. That realization was equivalent to the singing, for it could heal the condition of suffering by accepting the suffering itself.

When the ego is immature and cut off from the energies that would bring renewal, those energies become destructive. I was familiar with that condition. It created in me a kind of psychological stone-throwing. When I felt envy for what I didn't have, I was hurling stones — in my imagination — at others, at myself, and at the Self for my perceived abandonment. The black and white of it was brought out in the contrast between the melodious voices of the boys in the choir and the disastrous act of stoning. If I were only "a boy in the choir," I wouldn't be ready to take up the responsibility of my own "stone."

I had to realize that I was being forced by the unconscious to suffer the "stone" to become psychologically a more solidified personality. Jung interpreted the image of being stoned as synonymous with this suffering. This image is also related to the darkness and "earthly gold" that the alchemists had to transform. Furthermore, Jung saw psychological suffering, disfigurement, and resolution in their spiritual aspects as equivalent to fire.[61]

This leads into the second dream, which I consider a milestone, the jewel revealing its true self. I am certain it came as a result of my time alone to concentrate on the work.

> *There is an intense heat wave, and all the world is suffering.*
> *But in the center of the earth God has put an ice cave*
> *with one animal inside that was chosen to survive,*
> *and I am privileged to be down there with him.*

My reaction to this dream was as dramatic as my emotional response to finding the Mesopotamian artifact. I cried for a long time. The dream said that I was selected to be rescued from suffering, and that meant that God was there, acknowledging me and protecting me. It authenticated my conviction that psychological work, and love for the work that transforms, is the most important and enduring task I could be engaged in.

By staying alone to write I was facing the chaos of creativity directly, deliberately abandoning my outer-world relationships for the sake of the inner-world process. This cave was a protection in the midst of the intense heat of the ego's struggles. Caves were the first houses and most likely the first churches. Symbolic of the Great Mother, the cave is a powerful archetypal image. It is an inner shrine, a fundamental image of introversion. Being inside the cave is like heavenly containment. The cave was my shrine, and the inner animal was an image of the divine.

When the mother dies at birth there is an opening into a vast space[62] — not for a human mother but a divine one. In my earlier years of analysis the heat of creativity came over me so that I hardly knew what was happening to me. I reacted instinctively, followed its urgency to become manifest, but didn't have the strength to integrate it into my everyday life. The animal in the center of the hot earth was not available to me in those early years, but it nevertheless was present in my psyche. The animal there inside me made it possible to stay alone three weeks to honor the creative urge that wanted to be realized. It was reminiscent of the image of my mother who appeared in the heat of the ulcer and provided stability.

While writing about the cave, I remembered a dream I'd had in the early years of my analysis. I was in a cave and on one of its walls was a secret niche that contained gifts from my mother. That was probably the first dream about her that I ever had. At the time I was in my early thirties and taking care of a toddler. I was fully engaged in being a mother myself and didn't have the time to spend on my inner work, especially my artwork. But after this dream, and without my conscious intention, an impassioned rush of energy poured from me to give form to those creative gifts. I ran back and forth from my home to the store to get the supplies I needed.

This was the first time I followed the urge to create so spontaneously. It was not enough just to write about the secret niche dream. I had to involve as much of myself as possible. It was as if I had been taken over by a force that wouldn't let me go until I lived it out concretely. This absorption lasted about a week. I made a stuffed animal, a horse, out of old shirts; I made a little house out of small red Legos and mounted it on a platform with shrubbery around it; I made a golden lotus out of paper and a collage of colored stones in the shape of a mandala as a gift to my mother. And then it was over.

The heat in the more recent cave dream was like the intensity of that creative moment, but it also represented untamed instincts and untamed emotions — emotional upheaval on a personal level. In communing with the animal, one's spirit and soul can reignite the fire within, and a spiritual attitude helps bring in the balance. When

I was writing, I was in the cave with the sacred animal, and I was close to those instincts in a quiet way. Heat is related to fire and represents the active principle, the emotions that are close to consciousness. The cave and its coolness relate more to the nature of the unconscious. To give the dream a living reality, I painted the cave and its animal as a portrait of thanksgiving (fig. 25).

The image of the animal helped me develop an awareness of the living connection to my psychological center. The alchemist Michael Maier wrote: "The centre contains the 'indivisible point' which is simple, indestructible, and eternal."[63] It is what is constant in the fire. The alchemist Gerhard Dorn said: "[N]othing is more like God than the centre . . . ."[64] In alchemical language, the fire has within it the incorruptible being that symbolizes the Self that endures. Being firmly rooted in the center of myself in turn transported me into the eternal part of myself. Being in the cave was like being the phoenix that burns and is renewed by the flames. In this regard this dream is like a creation myth — the birth of a new consciousness.

Fig. 25: *I am communing with the animal in the cave.*

Concentrating on my inner work I was enduring the fires of transformation, and that meant it was again a psychologically dangerous time. Jung wrote about this new state of being that can be

> threatened on the one hand by the negative attitude
> of the conscious mind and on the other by the
> [devouring] unconscious, which is quite ready to
> swallow up all its progeny . . . . Nothing in all the
> world welcomes this new birth, although it is the
> most precious fruit of Mother Nature herself, the
> most pregnant with the future, signifying a higher
> state of self-realization. That is why Nature, the
> world of instincts, takes the "child" under its wing:
> it is nourished or protected by animals.[65]

The animal and the ancestors in the unconscious were alive inside me. I had been taken under their wing in childhood, long before I was conscious of their protective influence. They had come to me in another dream several years after the cave dream.

*I am in the fifth grade, and two Native American women are
watching over me.*

I had surgery on the scars on my upper arms when I was in the fifth grade. The dream told me that the Native American women offered me safekeeping. They shielded me from the negative influences I was facing. I needed these women, and they had been there, supporting and protecting me. Contrary to my desire to have the scars removed, they wanted me to keep the scars, not for further humiliation but, rather, for further protection. The two indigenous women from my own native soil, were guardians of my heart, ancestor archetypes in the deep unconscious. The supportive side of the psyche had sent these women to ensure my survival and further my progress in integrating the early trauma and its seemingly hopeless outcome. Years before this dream, I had portrayed my mother as an Indian woman in a healing painting, but my ego seemed perpetually caught by the literal mother's death and the continuing hope for her return.

My lifelong sadness had been repressed, and the full expression of it, so necessary for healing, had never occurred. It was not until I was in my late forties that it finally surfaced, and quite unexpectedly, just before my son left for college. We were sitting at the kitchen table, and he was talking about his plans and hopes for the future. Suddenly I realized that I hadn't had a mother to accompany me through the initiatory stages of life. At that thought, the long-repressed tears erupted from my core. Within seconds, my son's leaving home had brought up the wrenching grief about my own mother's leaving.

This time around, I was able to consciously hold the powerful impact of my loss. The deep sorrow that had been only an intellectual concept, became an intense reality. The family my husband and I had created with our son had provided a container for me, and I would miss the comfort it rendered. The long-overdue lament finally came out in the upwelling of my tears. It made room for a deeper healing and opened the way for the supportive mother-energy I had been longing for, which began to appear in unexpected places.

One example occurred after our son went away to college. My husband and I went on a holiday to initiate the new phase in our lives. A week into our vacation, as we sat in the restaurant of the lodge where we were staying, a family next to us captured my attention. I stared longingly at their interactions. They all seemed to be enjoying one another, parents and grandparents laughing with each other and with their little girl. She held up a lollipop and said to the waiter, "See what I have?" The waiter didn't acknowledge her as he was busy with the orders, but the little girl followed him with her eyes as he walked away. She was so secure within herself that she accepted this oversight. "How heavenly," I thought, "to be in a family so full of life, so related to themselves and to one another and to feel so contained." As I was watching this family, I observed myself yearning once again for the good-mother experience that this family represented.

The abandonment complex was waiting for a catalyst, and this fit the bill. My deepest feelings were stirred. Yet the gods were kind to me and took note of my despair. It was as if they knew I would need many living authentications of the good-mother experience, and to that end they created a synchronistic event. Our waiter that evening proved to be a good-mother in disguise. As it happened, we had sat at the same table the day before, discussing what we could and couldn't eat. This evening as I was looking at this family, our waiter told us he had overheard what we had said about the food the previous night and had thought about what he could have specially prepared for us that we could eat. There she was — the mother I had missed who really hears her child and tries to satisfy its hunger and needs. The abandoned orphan part of myself had been calling from the depths, and the mother reappeared in the waiter.

Another event offered further healing: our college-age son had an emergency appendectomy. The morning after the surgery my husband and I sat on opposite sides of his hospital bed, relieved that he was well and each holding our son's hand. In that moment a *déjà vu* feeling came over me. I relived the embrace of the parent and child I had felt so briefly with my mother and that had been so brutally taken away. Eighteen years earlier at my son's birth, the three of us relived another *déjà vu* of my own birth. I had been concerned for my husband's life following his illness; in spite of a successful childbirth and a healthy boy, I had been preoccupied with the death side of the equation. Now I was experiencing the life side, and the three of us were together to celebrate. There were echoes of my early traumatic event, but in this instance, life accompanied us. The benevolent mother was there, and I was able to reach her.

In spite of my increasing capacity to accept the early loss, underneath it all I still wanted to see my mother. I wanted to meet her and touch her. The painting of my mother and the active imagination in which she appeared in my ulcer inaugurated a new inner connection to her, but it just wasn't enough. Although that desire was irrational my psyche was preparing a path she could take to visit me: as close to a living experience of my mother's return as was humanly possible. As I was ending my analysis (five years after the active imagination when my mother appeared in my ulcer) the hoped-for reunion came about in a dream.

> *My mother comes across the lobby of a hotel to meet me.*
> *My mind is reeling with the exuberant thought:*
> *"Finally you have come!" We walk toward each other with powerful*
> *emotion, and we embrace. It is an unbelievable experience.*
> *I lead her into a lecture hall and sit down, and she sits behind me.*
> *I reach back, and we hold hands with a shared passion for this*
> *moment in time we have long awaited.*

I could hardly believe it. We actually met. The dream was alive with vibrancy. It was like an apparition, because it was undeniably my mother, just as she looked in my photographs of her. This remarkable event would make an indelible mark on my psyche. Because the dream came a month before I stopped analysis, I felt that she had come to accompany me in this new birth into a life on my own. But this time she was coming back — not leaving.

The reunion with my mother took place in a hotel, a place of transit outside my familiar surroundings. In such a place the psyche is particularly receptive to the other side. The room where we sat was one where I had heard a talk on cultural myth and healing rites years before. That talk had encouraged me to pursue the keloid material in a more concentrated way. The dream was showing me that my mother had come to support my research. When I began to follow this plan of study, the transpersonal realm greeted me with open arms. It was as if it was sending my mother as an envoy to encourage further pursuit of my work. Her image had come to me originally in the form of an Indian woman on the canvas. Then she appeared again when I went into the ulcer in the colon. Now she was one step closer.

After my excitement about her appearance and a deluge of tears, I knew things would have to be different, and I was at a loss as to what to do. My long-standing journey into the unconscious was beginning to yield fruit. Finding my mother was, at the same time, finding a connection to the living spirit within myself. I had to experience this spirit as separate from hers to make it my own. Now I would have to go on without the same intensity of longing to be with her. It would have to be replaced with something of equal numinosity.

Accepting the return of my mother into my psychological life was as difficult as considering getting pregnant had been twenty years earlier. So shocking was this return that I knew I would have to strengthen the bond with the unconscious, so that it would support a new life attitude. This bond would have to have an intensity equal to the crossing my mother had made. I reached for what had supported me in the past: I began an active imagination with a mother image, but not directly with my personal mother. The thought of talking to her directly was difficult. It was as if I needed an inner guide to give me permission to live with the return of my mother, to accept this gift. In that active imagination, I went to an old lady on the hill, and I told her that my whole life had been centered on how I missed having my mother close to me. I said, "I want to keep my mother alive inside me as she was in the dream. It is the only thing that can bring me alive."

The old lady said that I needed to develop complete trust in my association with her (the old lady). As we went to an innermost room,

I said I was frightened to be on my own, and now that my mother had returned, I would have to be accountable. Despite my initial enthusiasm, the darkness had crept in, and I wondered if I should go on at all. I wanted to stay with the old lady and not have to live out the reality of the dream. I was afraid I was going to die and afraid I was going to live. But it wasn't a literal death I faced; I could sense that. I knew I was in a transition, and that was why I was talking with her. She was to usher me into my next phase, in spite of my fear of life.

I said, "I feel the sweet promise of a mother when someone is here. And then they leave, and the sweet promise is gone. There was no one there to hold me. There was only darkness all around when I was initially alone. I was lost, confused and disoriented. When I remember it I am overcome. I don't ever want to be there again. I was paralyzed waiting for my mother to come back, and I am paralyzed now that she has come back. Life was death." She replied, *"Go all the way down into my center so I can hold you and you can be born again into a new world."* I climbed into her and curled up. It was as if I were going all the way back in time. The old woman asked me to go deeper still, and that meant to go inside myself and reveal my thoughts.

She said, *"You must write for yourself, not your mother, to keep yourself alive."* Then, as the old lady spoke, my mother suddenly appeared. I said to her, "I need you, Mother, so we can talk. I didn't know, before now, that I have something to say." She said, *"Maybe it's when you have someone to say it to."* "Mother, you are the living life for me. You are all I have. Our reunion is critical to me. I have to be with you. I can't get what I need anywhere else. I have to tell you how I suffer here without you. Even though I have to live my everyday life, I'll wait right here at the edge. I'm so afraid you'll disappear again." She said (to my surprise), *"I need to see you, too, and I will wait here."* I pictured myself standing at the edge of time waiting for her. For several days, while her essence was still around, I stood at the edge of the land of the living, and she stood at the edge of the land of the dead, and we met again and again. The intensity of the experience could not last, but it was engraved in my memory. I knew that I had to renew my dedication to living my own life so that we could continue meeting.

Psychologically, the image of the old lady on the hill was an image of the Self. It helped me endure the reality of what my mother's return in the dream portended: namely, a separation from my identity with the personal mother and the birth of a more conscious ego. Then I could relate to the Self on my own terms. It seemed that could only happen after I had had the immediate experience of my mother's return to me. For too many years I had thought I wasn't up to life's demands, so I had concentrated on preserving my mother's life as a defense against living my own life. Safeguarding her life had given me a role to play and a purpose for living, but it could be my purpose no longer.

To express this revelation I painted an image of my mother going off with Death. I had not fully descended into the painful memory of my literal birth and my mother's death until I painted it. I had no idea what would happen when I began to paint, though my unconscious had long held this picture deep inside. I was the only living figure in the painting, witnessing the traumatic event (fig. 26). After I completed the picture I wrote this poem and became totally immersed in reverie.

> As we lay in the hospital waiting
> For Death to come,
> To take you away from me,
>
> Turn you did to him
> and left
> Holding his hand - not mine.
>
> I lay in the hospital waiting
> for Death to come back for me.
>
> I tried to anticipate
> A life without you.
>
> Death had come and gone
> and left a scream,
>
> The leavings I would come to know
> and the terror I would feel
> all stemmed from that cry.
>
> I lay in the hospital
> relieved
> Death hadn't come for me.

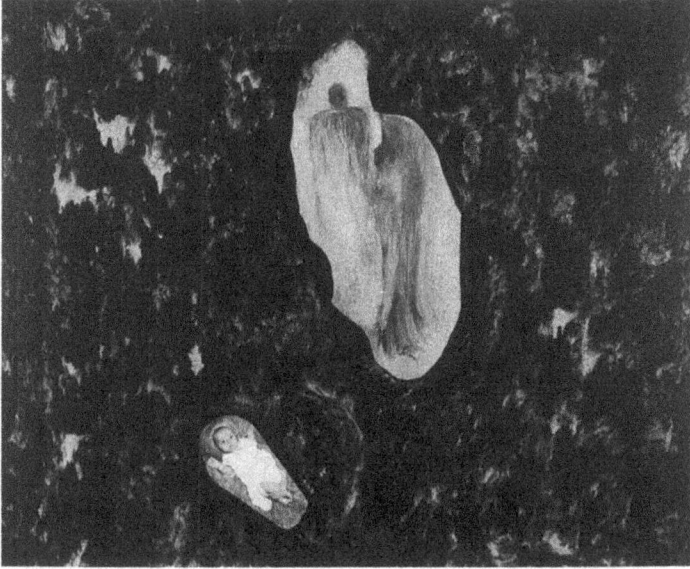

Fig. 26: *My mother going off with Death.*

Bringing this memory across the threshold from the unconscious, putting it on the canvas and expressing it in poetry affected me so deeply that my ego became possessed by a force beyond my control. Under its grip, I felt compelled to follow my mother into death. What transpired shows the potentially dangerous power of active imagination. After I had written a few paragraphs about following her into death, everything around me and inside me abruptly turned still. I could not move, and I could hardly breathe. This lasted only a few minutes, although it felt like an eternity. When it didn't shift, I felt caught, and I started to panic. Fortunately, just as suddenly as the stillness of death had come over me and, I feared, come for me, up came the thought: "My mother gave me her name. That meant she noticed me and that she did care about me after all." Somehow that realization immediately released me from the pull of the underworld, and I could feel the blood rushing through my veins again. I was reminded of the quote Jung often cited from the German poet, Hölderlin: "Where danger is, there / Arises salvation also."[66]

Doing active imagination can be dangerous if the ego is not strong enough or in the right place, and once into it, it is essential to know when to stop. When I did the painting of my mother going off with Death I couldn't psychologically hold the experience. There was a built-in allure about returning to the place where the creative meets the chaos, as happened when I did this painting. That is where one can fall into chaos, or be seduced in. When I followed my mother into the death place in active imagination, I was taking literally what needed to be understood psychologically. I needed to stay in the numinous experience of a death relived.

Active imagination can create a suspension in the spirit world, and that puts one at high risk as a target of the paradoxical forces in the psyche. For me, there was a subtle temptation to be reabsorbed into pure spirit, for that was where my mother resided. It was the place of our dream meeting, and it was tempting to stay there with her, the condition I had always wanted. But of course I couldn't. We had to be two separate individuals, she on her side and I on mine. It was now established in my mind that she had a place in her own world.

The death pull that came up in me after the painting was yet another example of the dark force rushing in to compromise new levels of consciousness. But the releasing thought that came across the threshold, just as my mother had come across the threshold to meet me, was an antidote to being caught in the netherworld. To help me hold onto the effects of that releasing message and to keep my mother's essence close to me, I returned to the easel to give tangible form to this experience in a more permanent way. A painting of us together would represent the culmination of the process that had just taken place. My mother had made the crossing in my dream, and I could reciprocate by painting a picture that would portray my search for her and her return to me. I began looking for a photograph of myself and one of her that, when put together, would look as if we were holding hands.

As I cut out and prepared the two photographs, I was carving us into the same time and space. I was enveloped again in a kind of mist. It was late at night by this time, and I put the photos on the table in my room. The energy coming from them was so intense and I was so excited that I couldn't sleep all night, nor could I get up and put them on the canvas. They sat on the table for several days before I could even approach them.

While I waited for the propitious moment (knowing a commitment would be required once the painting was complete), I reviewed what I understood about what had happened thus far. I found my mother by going as deeply into myself as I could. Psychologically, in bringing her into my world, I was making possible an active relationship with the part of me she represented. My identification with my mother was loosening, and I was gaining a more objective relationship to her. No longer shrouded by the death complex, I was giving up the illusion of its protection. The identification with my mother had become my universe. When she vanished, my world had vanished with her. Acknowledging this reality, I was then able to prepare our pictures for their new place on the canvas of my life (fig. 27).

As fate would have it, there was yet another level for me to reach to solidify my relationship with my mother. It announced itself about a year after this dream of my mother's return and came through a patient who told me a myth about the birth of the Indian god Krishna. The story presents the theme of danger accompanying new birth. A nursemaid was sent by Krishna's father, the king, and instructed to poison the new baby Krishna to prevent him from growing up and replacing the king. Upon finding the baby, the nursemaid put poison on her nipples and began to nurse him. But Krishna *didn't* die; rather, he became

Fig. 27: *My mother and me.*

110

stronger and stronger, and after he had sucked out all her milk the nursemaid died. Krishna lived on, and the old king was overthrown.[67]

This story affected me deeply as a symbolic representation of what I believed my mother and I were involved in. Immediately I connected it to my underlying guilt in relation to my mother, as if she had died because I had sucked out all of her milk (her life force). The destructive forces reminded me of their presence, for when I first heard this myth I felt the familiar despair. Seen through the eyes of the complex, I was once again personally responsible for bringing on the death. But the myth also brought in a new twist; my mother's death could have been necessary for my survival. It hadn't occurred to me that she could have been a sacrifice so I could live. The thought of being important enough to have someone's death ensure my survival (objectively speaking, the survival of life) was a big piece to swallow. It would mean that I had to appreciate my own value and not project it incessantly on my mother, or on my parents' relationship.

There were many levels of the experience of the death to be absorbed. On the one hand I would never really know why my mother died. I was merely a part of that event. Yet I was trying to define her dying solely as a part of my equation. Declaring "I am such and so because she died" was quite different from "I am such and so *and* she died." Seen in this light, the suffering of my life was not a punishment for her death. It was a part of my own life process and her life process. This view incorporated more of my mother's psyche and put it in a more comprehensive perspective. When my mother went off alone into death and I went off alone into life, she had been orphaned from me, too.

The story of Krishna and my ruminations on our separate myths had such a profound effect that my mother came back in a second dream.

> *My mother stood by my bedside.*
> *She was naked and showed me she had a third*
> *nipple on top of her breast that was shriveled.*
> *Then she turned around and walked away.*

My first thought upon awakening was that my mother had come back again in this dream to authenticate the naked truth: the third nipple signifies what really did happen to us psychologically. Also, the dream was corroborating my insights, and now that they had become conscious, the purpose of her initial visit had been fulfilled, and she could walk away. Seen more objectively, a larger naked truth had been proclaimed: the old must die for the new to be born and for life to triumph. The myth and my dream reiterated the theme of the treacherous period surrounding the hero's birth, when negative forces want to do away with new life. In my earliest dream this was represented by the tree without leaves that could have portended my own barrenness had the life urge not been so strong.

Another example of the continuing challenge of darkness was in the consequences of carrying the blame for her death: it was like being blamed for the demise of the Self that my mother represented. I had carried the projection of the intractable part of the unconscious that challenges new life. It is a huge burden — and a great error — when the ego takes as personal what belongs to the gods. Nature had arranged that the dark side should come in with new birth, and I could no longer feel guilty for things I hadn't even been conscious of.

One other piece of the darkness had grabbed me: by identifying with Krishna's birth, I became special. I had survived in the face of another's death. Not having a "life" mother was a divine birth, and I associated it with Christ not having a "life-father," and with Buddha, whose mother died within seven days after his birth. My potential omnipotence was quickly dashed by the mere thought of having to live up to the responsibilities this divine role would entail. I just wanted to be an ordinary mortal again.

My sense of entitlement was not new and had long been entrenched in a negative inflation that made me fear that having caused one death I could cause others. A dark force had suckled me and its poison had come inside me. Jung explained it this way:

> The hero's birth and the heroic life are always threat-
> ened. The serpents sent by Hera to destroy the infant
> Hercules, the python that tries to strangle Apollo at
> birth, the massacre of the innocents, all these tell the
> same story. To develop the personality is a gamble,
> and the tragedy is that the daemon of the inner voice
> is at once our greatest danger and an indispensable
> help. It is tragic, but logical, for it is the nature of
> things to be so.[68]

As the years passed, I had to remain as conscious as possible of these dual forces, but it felt as if the negative side was releasing some of its hold on my psyche and allowing the positive side to let its presence be known. Miraculously I had made it to the place where my mother and I could meet. With this experience of grace the orphan wound closed a little bit more.

There were many ways to continue to nurture my mother's closeness. My work on the scars' meaning was the major one. When I gave public talks, in both preparing and delivering them, I felt as if she were there, and I felt like her daughter. The work made me stronger, and I was as I had imagined her to be. At those times I was completely at one with her and with myself. The scars were powerfully numinous to me, especially because they represented both this life and the Beyond. Only what caused me to go inside to find its meaning could bring in the mother and bridge this world and the next. The scars had done that. Now, in turning my full attention to studying them I found a new reason to live.

# CHAPTER SEVEN

# THE KELOID SEEKS ME

*[F]or the neophyte, it would be a real sin if he shrank from the torture of initiation. The torture inflicted on him is not a punishment but the indispensable means of leading him towards his destiny.*[69]

My mother had several times appeared to me, but the research I was about to begin would create a more prominent path not only to her, but also for her to take to me. Perseverance in the work would also solidify a path for the eternal spirit that had created the keloid and safeguarded its continuation. It was becoming evident that there was a connection between the scars and my mother. A spiritual perspective insured my access to this connection.

I began my study of the keloid by exploring its physiology. What I learned in reviewing the medical literature[70] is that ordinary scar tissue, at first red and raised above the surrounding skin, fades and begins to shrink slightly with age. Keloids, by contrast, result from a proliferation of scar tissue and grow beyond the site of the original injury. They are autonomous overgrowths of scar tissue. Elevated, irregularly-shaped, progressively enlarging scars, they develop a shiny, smooth, taut surface and a hard consistency due to excess collagen formation. There is a genetic predisposition for this to occur. Keloids evolve as a result of a trauma; the initial wound can be as serious as a severe burn or cut, or as trivial as an acne lesion.

The first clinical description of the keloid was made by Louis Alibert in 1814.[71] He originally called it "cancroid," later changing the name to "cheloid" or keloid. The name is derived from the Greek word meaning "claw" because extensions into the neighboring tissues often resemble the claws of a crab. Keloids are generally one specific growth but may occur in multiple tumors varying in size and shape, mostly located on the upper back, chest, breasts, earlobes and on abdominal incisions. They are benign but produce irritating symptoms such as itching, tenderness, intermittent smarting pain, skin discoloration, and cosmetic disfigurement. Keloids are more common in darker-skinned races with a higher incidence in younger individuals, occurring more frequently during puberty and pregnancy, perhaps from hormonal influence.[72]

Treatments to remove or reduce keloids have met with variable success. Each condition is very individual, and the patient is usually informed about the probable amount of improvement so as not to raise unrealistic expectations. The most common treatments are excisional surgery combined with other procedures, such as radiation therapy, topical and intralesional corticosteroids, pressure devices, and topically applied silicone gel sheeting. Some keloids are amenable to laser treatment. Significant improvement of keloid symptoms has resulted from these various treatments, yet recurrence or worsening can also happen. Keloids are persistent; "[l]ike the Hydra of Greek legend, this is the keloid which grows two heads each time one is excised."[73]

Researchers have defined structure, function, and biochemical factors in keloid formation, but their etiology is unknown. Though true keloids rarely arise spontaneously, it is my hypothesis that psychic injuries can result in keloid formation. My own experience with keloids indicates that they do emerge on the skin in a "spontaneous" fashion and that psychological wounds may be the precipitating factor. I believe that psychic experiences can generate physiological effects, including hormonal imbalance and immunological deficiencies; persons predisposed to keloid formation can produce a lesion resulting in keloid growth as a consequence of wounding psychic experiences.

In modern dermatology texts, keloids are not mentioned among skin diseases with a probable psychogenic component. Yet a few medical researchers and writers have been conscious of the possibilities of such a relationship. One physician expresses his wonder at the keloid's recurrence: "It seems so reasonable to excise [keloids] and so unreasonable that they should return bigger than ever."[74] A subtitle in a French article on keloids suggests the writers' awareness that the origin of the keloid may be connected to some aspects beyond the merely physical: "The Undesirable Skin Scar: Punishment or Destiny?"[75] Another dermatologist makes this concession to the subjective element: "Although keloids do have a life cycle, it is one measured in decades. Hence, no one can expect our patient to view her progressively disfiguring scar as a self-limiting spontaneously resolving process. She needs treatment but assuredly not surgical!"[76] And a Nigerian physician writing on the origins and history of divination among the Ifa, a cult of the Yorubas, appreciates the role of divine intervention:

"[The Ifa priests] also knew that once a lesion appears it grows in size and has no remedy except when the Divine power is suitably appropriated to intervene in bringing about its resolution."[77]

These suggestions of a possible relationship between the physical keloid scar and a spiritual process led me to explore the symbolic dimension of scars. My research began with an African tale told by a writer and long-time friend of Jung's, Laurens van der Post. It is an excellent illustration of retrieving what is lost by making a descent into darkness. The myth is about a beautiful young girl who, taunted by her jealous sisters, loses her beads in a deep pool. When she descends into the pool to retrieve them, she comes upon an old woman with one leg and one arm and with hideous sores and burns all over her body. The old woman says, "Laugh at me," but the young girl can't do that. The old woman then asks her to lick her wounds and sores, and in spite of the young girl's revulsion, she licks the wounds. This old woman happens to be the cook for a one-eyed monster who devours human beings. When the monster returns, the old woman hides the girl out of gratitude for her willingness to lick her sores. The monster smells the human flesh and burns the old woman all the more. The next morning he goes out, and because the young girl has had compassion for her, the old woman returns her beads and rewards her with fine clothing and jewels. The girl then becomes "the mother of a great nation." When she returns home her sisters, who at first hardly recognize her because she is so beautifully dressed, become envious and, wanting equal bounty, descend into the pool. But they refuse to have anything to do with the old woman, let alone lick her sores. So they are devoured by the one-eyed monster.[78]

In this tale, the beautiful young girl (the ego) has to submit to forces greater than herself by descending into the unknown waters (the unconscious) and experiencing (in this case tasting) the darkness in order to retrieve what is lost (her intended identity). In descending into the water, the young girl meets the wounded aspects of herself in the form of the old woman with sores. Both wounding and healing are ingredients here. The old woman represents the eternal wound of suffering, as if it were living beneath the surface of the waters of the psyche.

Relating to the maimed old woman inside oneself, the one who bears the sores and wounds of life, can offer protection from the darkness, the one-eyed monsters within and without. The old wounded woman cooked for the one-eyed monster, yet she could offer protection and initiation to others in need. She represents the regenerating aspect of making a conscious relationship to the monster (in the inner and outer world). Cooking for it, so to speak, provides new life. The sisters, who were envious and uncaring and who refused to lick the sores of the old woman, were unable to partake in the regenerating aspect and were consequently devoured. The beads represent the inner value with which the young girl has temporarily lost touch (the spirit in matter that needs to be retrieved and the lost substance embedded in the unconscious). By licking the wounds of the old woman, she reclaims it. Licking the sores paralleled images in my own dreams of eating the scars as grapes, eating the goldfish raw and swallowing the snake.

Descending into the depths and following the body symptom down to its inception one meets the pain of its passage into being, i.e. one meets the old woman with sores that need tending. She stands between the ego and the monster. If the descent is made under kind and benevolent eyes (the right psychological attitude) and if the diver's intention is "of the highest virtue," healing is more likely. If one descends through the layers of the psyche and the body, down to the chaos at the moment of creation, one may find renewal.

The individuation process, with its recurring descents into the unconscious for renewal, offers a continuing reenactment of creation. It is a hero's journey and a night sea journey and, as Jung remarks, "[D]arkness precedes the light and is its mother."[79] Descending into the depths and having to lick one's own wounds is also descending into one's deepest feelings, to the unsightly sores of the underside of things. There the monster resides, and there redemption is possible.

This African myth set the stage for enlarging my comprehension of the scars. My continued study led me to Jung's *Answer to Job*. I began to understand more fully what was meant when God was tempted by Satan to test Job's loyalty by, among other things, inflicting disease upon his body[80] (fig. 28). Job's plight could be understood psychologically as an initiation process, as the Self's breaking up the ego's status quo to bring about a new level of development in Job and in his relationship with God. The message of this story inspired me to go beyond the wounds of my early life and once again to enter the depths of the symptom where the divine spirit dwelled.

Through active imagination I began: "I hear the souls, screaming in pain, who have no home. Who will carry them? Their anguish is almost

Fig. 28: *Disease as a scourge of God (woodcut by Hans Wechtlin, Strassburg, Germany, sixteenth century A.D., published in 1517 by Hans Gersdorff,* Die Krankheitsdarstellungen*).*

more than I can bear. These souls are encased in scars, bearing heavy burdens. Their collective voice represents eons of anguish. The souls are screaming to be freed from their imprisonment in the scars. Encapsulated in the scars, their screams reach through to me." It was as if the souls wanted me to recognize them so that I could communicate what they are. The scars in the active imagination spoke for these souls.

> *We are an accumulation of people's neglect and are lost in space. Pay attention to what we say. We will not say it twice. You need to protect us now. We are raw and out of our container. We trust you to protect and absorb more and more of our value. We have been tears over centuries, for blame and guilt are a shrine people use as an excuse for their life's work. Blame and guilt have been thrown at us because people don't want to transform us. If you work with us you'll have nothing to fear. We are not beautiful. Locked in your own prejudices you avoid hearing us. You are afraid of responsibility, but you will never not know us now. You are not innocent. You demand perfection, but you are a part of us.*

The scars were calling out for me to hear what they represented collectively and personally. They wanted me to protect them as they had protected me. I hoped to meet this need by consciously carrying the suffering of the collective wound. It would give my personal suffering a far greater meaning and purpose and make it easier to bear.

In the active imagination the scars told me that I had to comprehend the principle of opposites at work in the psyche. I returned to my dreams and visions to extract more of their essential message. The specific symbols were relevant to me personally, but their directive had a universal reality. I drew on images from the earlier dreams: in order to know the singing, I had to know that darkness exists; to know the fruit, I had to swallow the snake; to get the key, I had to endure the dark mother; to live I had to know death; to know God, I had to meet the tiger and experience the heat; to paint, I had to know the imprisonment in the tower and the confines of the Self, to which one is limited; and to be rescued from the blame, I had to testify to the truths as I became conscious of them. The keloids also spoke to this level; they did not want to be seen as merely scar tissue.

The keloids were a continuing reflection of my psychological changes. The scars had caused me pain, but they provided protection from the volatility of the unconscious. They were insisting on a transformation into what was more evolved in me. The life force inside me that created the scars and was projected onto the scars also led me to discover the art of scarification. As I became more psychologically developed, their higher side, manifested through the art of scarification, was shown to me. The research on scarification would lead to the expansion of the cultural dimension in my life. Up to that point the scars had been merely a personal matter. Now, my view of them began to change.

Because the scars represented a vital part of my existence, exploring their historical and cultural dimension would ground me in the larger universe and plant my feet solidly on the earth. The scars' historical base incorporated culture, art, medicine and psychology. My work on the metaphysical level of the keloid would expand and enlarge not only my world view but also my way of being in the world. I needed to synthesize my regressive longings for my mother and incorporate them into a much broader perspective.

One keloid dream in particular supported this creative work.

*A man is standing on the sidewalk corner talking to some women about*
*his keloid that has grown where his penis had been removed.*
*He has a new penis in his hand. It is large and powerful.*
*I pass by and overhear the word "keloid" as he is proudly showing it,*
*and I want to tell him that the penis has the thinnest skin of any area*
*of the body and that's why it is the most sensitive.*
*He thinks that is very interesting.*

In this dream the keloid substitutes for the creative organ, the principal
fertility symbol. The keloid's connection to the penis represents its
function of transforming libido, the death and rebirth of creative energy. Creativity integrates the phallic aspect, the masculine side of the
woman's psyche, and the role of this phallic aspect in her inner world.
The keloid inspired my creativity and my active relationship to the
psyche. If my interactions with the unconscious were assimilated on
the conscious level, creative work would give me a new attitude,
helping me overcome my view of myself as limited. The sensitivity
may refer to my being sensitive about revealing my scars, their representing my limitations, but may also stand for the deepest layers of
my psyche, born from the wound and discovered through creative
work. In order to bring the message of the keloid into a living reality
I needed to concentrate my research on the archetype of the keloid
and its relevance in my life.

The keloid research was imperative for me as an orphan, who, like
the hero, must continually leave lesser stages of development once
they are recognized and outgrown and move on to the next (or higher)
levels where one stands on one's own. What Jung said made me realize that this wouldn't mean I would be all alone in the world. "It is . . .
only in the state of complete abandonment and loneliness that we
experience the helpful powers of our own natures."[81] Furthermore, he
explains that the fundamental passage of leaving a "lesser stage to
move to a higher one" is "to obtain transformation from the concrete,
the material into the unseen, the spiritual."

> [T]he great *principle of transformation* [begins]
> *through the things that are lowest* . . . that hide from the
> light of day and from man's enlightened thinking,
> hold also the secret of life, that renews itself again
> and again, until at last, when man understands, he

may grasp the inner meaning which has been till then hidden within the very texture of the concrete happening. In the past when a transformation of this kind was sought, the mystery religions prescribed a ritual of initiation.[82]

The keloid was the concrete happening, and each step I took on my journey to explore its hidden meaning was a ritual of initiation. Investigating the ancestral background of the scars was an integral part. It created the path to a larger realm and deepened my acquaintance with my own ancestral roots. My research turned out to be the initiation I needed.

I soon discovered, through books and articles in anthropology and art on the subject of body decorations, scarification, and tattooing, that the keloid scar had its own myth which merged with my own. It was as if the scars were reaching beyond the mother all the way back to the beginning of the first recorded images of woman. Between 20,000 and 15,000 B.C., in Paleolithic times, statues of goddesses were carved, and they had markings incised on their bodies (fig. 29).[83]

The practice of making raised keloidal body markings has apparently existed in many places for over 4,000 years. Otzi, the iceman who died

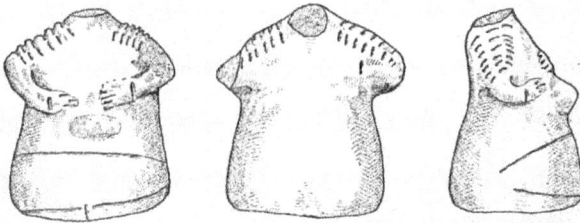

Fig. 29: *Statues of goddesses in Paleolithic times had markings incised on their bodies. Personal communication from Marija Gimbutas.*

in an Alpine blizzard some 5,000 years ago and whose preserved body was found in the Italian South Tyrol in 1991, had several tattoos.[84] The decorations on female figurines in predynastic Egypt, in the 4th millennium B.C., are thought by some to represent tattoos.[85] Figurines with cicatrice (scar tissue)-like markings dating from the end of the 7th millennium B.C. were found in Achilleion, Thessaly, in northern Greece (fig. 30).[86] Similar pellets of clay appeared on sculptures found in western Mexico, in tombs of a civilization that flourished around 1800 B.C. (fig. 31).[87] Archaeologists have also found Nigerian terracotta heads from the city-state of Ife, dating from the twelfth century A.D., that

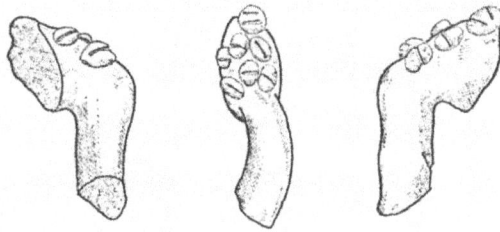

Fig. 30: *Arm fragments from ancient figurines, 7th millennium B.C., Achilleion, Thessaly in northern Greece. Personal communication from Marija Gimbutas.*

Fig. 31: *Pellets of clay on sculptures found in western Mexico tombs. From my personal collection.*

Fig. 32: *Nigerian terracotta head from the city-state of Ife that depicts grooved scarification, twentieth century reproduction. From my personal collection.*

depict facial scarification (fig. 32).[88] The art of body marking is old, practiced most frequently by African tribes and by the aborigines of Australia and Polynesia.

Two Nigerian legends tell a tale about the keloid's beginnings. The first one is relevant because it is about a man who did not know his mother before she died. In this story, the scars were at first associated with punishment and then later were admired and sought after.

> [T]he distinguishing marks on the arms of the members of the royal family of Oyo started after the funeral rites of Shango's mother. Shango did not know his mother before she died so he sent two of his slaves, one Hausa and one Yoruba, to go and sacrifice to her in Nupeland where she was buried and instructed them that they should listen carefully to whatever names his mother's kinsmen would call her during the ceremony. The Yoruba slave listened and remembered the name on their return to their master, while the Hausa slave was reveling when the ceremony was

on and could not tell Shango the name. As a punishment, the Hausa slave was whipped until he was bleeding all over the body. When the cuts healed, the scars were so attractive that Shango's wives did not only admire them on the slave but insisted that such marks were too beautiful to find on a slave; they should be given to their children.[89]

The second story involved "a man who had two wives but he loved one more than another. One day a crocodile was caught and placed in the room of the wife whom he did not love. The wife saw it and admired the patterns on its back so she took it to the blacksmith and asked him to cut the same patterns on her body. After the operation, the marking was so good that other women started to copy it."[90] Psychologically, the unloved wife's seeking the markings in order to change her dark state of affairs results in transformation. Her difficult circumstances mark her, but they also give her an individual status.

The practice of placing scars on the body had a multitude of meanings. Scarification has been performed as an art form — to beautify, to decorate, and to mark initiation and times of transitions. The scars were made for identification (fig. 33), to establish precise status, and

Fig. 33: *The marks on this woman from Bagassi were made for purposes of identification.*

Fig. 34: *Group of men and women in mourning. Reprinted from* The Northern Tribes of Central Australia *by Baldwin Spencer and F. J. Gillen: London, Macmillan & Co., 1904, fig. 148, p. 538.*

to prevent individuals' being taken into slavery. They represent proof of accomplishment, times of mourning (fig. 34), health states (fig. 35), and relationships to royalty, the ancestors, and the gods. Body decoration is vital to many celebrations, such as marriage, childbirth, and rites of renewal. Dark pigmentation lends itself to sculpting the skin in high relief. Tattooing is better suited to light skin. Scarification is usually performed on dark-skinned people.[91]

Scarification rites are performed on specific occasions in the lives of tribal members. In order for these rites to have a full and lasting effect on the initiate, the body must be ritually marked. Initiation ceremonies (fig. 36) are the most commonly known rituals associated with scarification and celebrate the rite of transformation, rebirth and the continuity of life. Initiation rites are frequently accompanied by circumcision, subincision, tooth extraction, etc. As part of the ceremony, the initiate commits him/herself to upholding the social patterns and beliefs of the group. In this new relationship to the collective, the individual carries more weight and is a more active participant in the group. The mystery involved in the ceremony, preparation, period

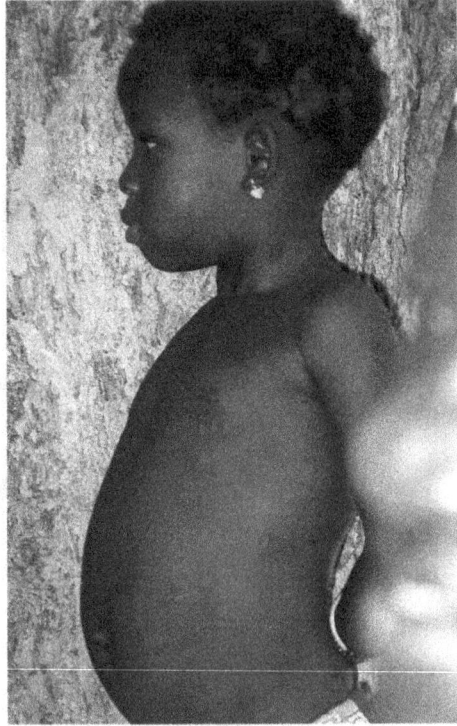

Fig. 35: *Scarification for healing on a child from Dogona.*

of solitude, and festivities following the scarifications testify to the event's sacredness.

Those who practice scarification believe that lessons will not be forgotten if they are inculcated at a time of extreme emotional tension and stress; for this reason body operations performed at initiations are painful and often bloody. They help the initiate develop courage and learn to endure suffering without complaint, and scars become permanent proof of her/his fitness and endurance. The shedding of blood is thought to be more tribally binding than any oath. Scarification is an indication of the initiate's new status among his fellow tribesmen.

In the Nuba, every female undergoes several scarification rituals, the first when she is ten or eleven years old, the second some time after the beginning of menstruation. Subsequent scarifications are made after her first child is weaned. She may receive a new design with each pregnancy. These scarifications have an erotic component and are associated with fertility. The more three-dimensional the scars become, the more desirable she is.[92]

Fig. 36: *Scarification for initiation. Reprinted from* People of Kau *by Leni Riefenstahl: New York, Harper and Row, 1976, © Leni Riefenstahl, by permission of Leni Riefenstahl - Produktion.*

The process of actually making the keloid scars begins with rubbing oil onto the parts of the body to be incised and tracing a line where the incisions will be made. Then a portion of the flesh is opened with a thorn or knife and an irritating juice is injected or ash, earth or charcoal is rubbed into the wound, allowing it to swell. Some wounds are opened many times to enlarge them. When the incisions have been made and the irritant injected, the wounds are dusted with a powder of roots and herbs which helps ease the pain and protect the wound from infection. The rite has its risks, even beyond infection. Disfigurement can develop, and a woman can lose a great deal of blood during the operation. Some lose consciousness. But to the initiate, the end result is worth the price as the scars render her highly attractive, desirable and, in effect, a sacred object.[93]

An example of scarification in male initiation rites comes from the aborigines of Australia. In these secret rites, the initiates go through three steps, each representing an epoch in their societal life. At the age of fourteen or fifteen, they enter the first stage. Little is known of this ceremony except that the novices are required to paint their faces black and speak in whispers. They advance to the second stage and undergo circumcision. The last and most important ceremony is at eighteen or twenty years of age when scarification takes place. At this point they are given the names that they will henceforth bear. Each name must be totally new, never having been used by any other person, alive or dead. Their bodies are scarred with quartzite fragments.

Fig. 37: *This Banutshu girl from the Belgian Congo undergoes cicatrization at the onset of her first menstruation. Reprinted from* The Body Decorated *by Victoria Ebin: London, Thames and Hudson, 1979, plate 58, by permission of the Royal Geographical Society, London.*

At the climax of the ritual, several of the older men open veins in their own arms, and the initiates swallow the first drops of blood. Next they prostrate themselves, and their backs are covered with a thick coat of blood which is allowed to congeal. One man marks with his thumb the places on their backs where incisions are to be made. Though great pain is inflicted, the initiates do not utter a sound or move a muscle. Drumming and singing often accompany these ceremonies to invoke the spirits, but also as a distraction for the initiate and to encourage him to endure the pain.[94]

Not only the existence but also the placement of scars can carry specific meaning. For example, among the Banutshu of the Congo, when a girl undergoes cicatrization at the onset of her first menstruation, the design consists of little dots cut on the upper part of her chest and breasts (fig. 37).[95] By contrast, among the Tiv, a tribe in central Nigeria, the abdomen may be scarified when a girl reaches puberty or when she expects her first child (fig. 38). It has been suggested that the lines

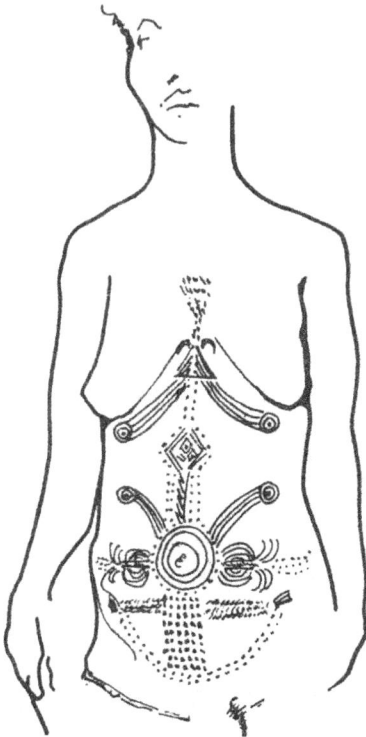

Fig. 38: *Among the Tiv, a tribe in central Nigeria, the abdomen may be scarified when a girl reaches puberty or when she expects her first child. Reprinted from fig. 16, "Women's Scarification, 'Swallow' Pattern," p. 49 in* Emerging from the Chrysalis: Studies in Rituals of Women's Initiation *by Bruce Lincoln: Cambridge, Massachusetts, Harvard University Press, 1981, based on a photograph in Charles F. Rowe, "Abdominal Cicatrisations of the Munshi Tribe, Nigeria," in* Man *(1928), vol. 28, pp. 179-180, at p. 179.*

in the abdominal designs may represent the woman's genealogical lineage, her ancestral heritage, land and tradition, passed on from generation to generation. The circle may represent the ripples on the pond with the past, present and future circling around the navel as axis.[96] For the Luba of Zaire, "Bodily transformations such as scarification . . . render a woman an effective vessel with which to capture and hold potent energies, and thereby establish direct communication with the spirit world."[97]

Creating these scars as art forms keeps alive the myths and philosophies of the ethnic group, as well as the connections to the group's ancestors. The Nuba believe that without their distinctive scars, they will not be admitted by their ancestors in the aftertime. The keloids are the messages of their forbearers; the marks upon the skin are their words.[98] In the Sun Dance, celebrated by the Native American peoples of the Great Plains, participants pierce themselves as part of a religious rite. "The Oglala holy man Black Elk stressed the mystic significance of the ordeal. 'As we thus break loose,' he said, 'it is as if we were being freed from the bonds of the flesh.'"[99] The Ga'anda of Northeast Nigeria, according to anthropologist Marla Burns, feel that positive spirit intervention ensures "that the patterns created are correct.[100] . . . [B]y altering the surfaces. . . the Ga'anda can localize and thereby ensure the cooperation of potentially dangerous and unpredictable forces."[101] Among the Tuareg people, henna is applied to bridegrooms' hands and feet as "an effective repellent of evil forces."[102] The Ewe of Togo and Ghana dust yam harvesters' faces, necks, feet, arms, chests and the backs of hands with white chalk powder for protection from "evil forces in the forest."[103] The Ekoi of Africa believed that in the next world scars can be exchanged for food "and that the ghost is able to remove them one by one for this purpose."[104] It has been noted that "the Fijian women who have not these marks [tattoos] are said to be served up as food for the gods."[105]

Scarification was performed in early times to protect people from being sold into slavery, because the disfigurement was disagreeable to Western whites and made people less valuable as slaves. Production of scars often accompanies mourning. Like self-wounding or flagellation, it was a way to bring back to memory someone who died. Aboriginal women showed their grief by scoring themselves with the sharp end of a digging stick or club when mourning for the dead.[106] They cut themselves until blood flowed to convey proper grief to the spirit that was hovering nearby. The scars were also made as protection against the death spirits returning for the living (fig. 39).

Fig. 39: *Scars as a sign of mourning. Reprinted from photo by E.L. Mitchell, plate XXXVIII in* The Psychology of a Primitive People: Study of the Australian Aborigine *by Stanley Porteus, originally published in 1931 by Edward Arnold & Co., London, and reprinted in 1977 by Ayer Company Publishers, Inc. of Manchester, NH, by permission of Ayer Company Publishers, Inc.*

In Polynesia, according to Waitz and Gerland, the deity to whom the person was dedicated could be identified by the patterns of the scars. The cut is the sign of the god to whom one belongs, one's personal protective spirit-god and the god of the tribe. The god descended upon the one with his sign, who was sanctified through this entry.[107] Every design is different to permit the spirits to reach each person. Uniqueness, as represented by individual scarification, ensures recognition by the gods; the scars serve as an antenna to receive their cosmic waves.[108] Tattoos are commonly found on the Maori people even today. The lines on the face can tell of deeds of heroism, successful and dangerous hunts; the tattooed spirals tell the story of the bearers' lives and genealogy.[109]

Inuit were tattooed to indicate that they had killed a polar bear, a walrus, or a whale. The tattoo then protected them from the spirit world while on the hunt and *after* the hunt against revenge from the spirit of the animal (or person) that they had killed. Tattoos reflected the Inuit's accomplishments and shielded him or her from perilous supernatural powers.[110]

Tattoos are often made with sharp instruments — thorns, bone, glass, stone and in modern times, electric tools. The Inuit drew a colored thread, blackened with soot, through the skin.[111] In general, body painting and tattooing (such as these) were performed to prevent old age and illness or to relate to guardian spirits. In British New Guinea the marks were made to acknowledge the killing of others. If a Bantu killed a man, a design was made from one eyebrow to another; in Borneo, the thigh was marked for the taking of a head.[112] At the beginning of the twentieth century German and Austrian men created a cult of the dueling scar, marking their social status.[113]

Tattoos and scarification were also used on slaves in the early Roman Empire as a punishment. The punitive application of tattoos was used by the Athenians against their captives on the Aegean island of Samos[114] in the sixth century B.C. and was also used in Japan in 400 A.D.[115] In Asia, tattooing goes back centuries.[116] Japanese figures such as dragons, birds, or flowers recall patterns on their silk fabrics. At first conferring dignity to the naked body, these designs were later picked up by the commercial middle class, who turned to tattooing when they weren't allowed to wear the finery of the elite. Foreigners — from heirs to the British and Russian thrones to American sailors — have been impressed by

Japanese tattoos and wanted to have them, and now one sees body tattoos everywhere.

Scarification as an ascetic practice for cultivating piety is centuries old. Circumcision was considered by some early people to be a symbolic sacrifice to a specific deity.[117] In the beginning, Semite circumcision was a sacrifice to the goddess of fertility; later it was a covenant between the people of Israel and Yahweh.[118] Herodotus reported that in a temple of Hercules in Egypt, "runaway slaves who took refuge in it were not liable to be re-captured if they had received on their bodies stigmata which signified their devotion to him."[119] Pontius in the third century "refers to Christian 'confessors whose foreheads were sealed with a (sacred) inscription.'"[120]

The etymology of the word "scarification" is best illustrated in the language of the Tabwa people of Southeast Zaire, which has been described by Allen Roberts.[121] According to Roberts, the Tabwa word *kulemba* encompasses the rich and varied meanings of the art of scarification.

> *Kulemba* means to inscribe and render meaningful an otherwise blank or incomprehensible surface or situation. . . to scarify, to draw or paint, design . . . in or on something especially so as to be conspicuous and durable. . .to perfect the human body through a system of signs . . . . [It also means] to put out new leaves and to succeed, reach a goal, catch a hunted game. After contact with literate coastal Swahili and European colonizers, the definition of *kulemba* was extended to include 'to write'. . . . Nouns derived from the verb root -*lemba* refer not only to scarification, writing and other inscriptions but also to successful hunters and perhaps to the Supreme Being.[122]

When I began to synthesize what I had learned and how it related to me personally, the amplification of scarification deepened the meaning of my spontaneous scars. During transitional events in my life the keloid archetype arose spontaneously in my body, just as in traditional cultures these marks were deliberately carved onto the body at the times of initiation. The archetypes of initiation, transformation, identification, and belonging presented themselves to the indigenous people and to me in the form of the keloid scar. When I successfully entered a new level of life — going to school, marriage, motherhood — my own scars appeared, individualizing the body by carving a design that held both personal and transpersonal meaning. My orphan psyche had been suspended in the transpersonal dimension, and my ego had never been fully realized. With the coming of the keloid, that began to shift.

From my research I found authentication of the fact that, whether purposefully made or spontaneous, scarification elicits the natural transformative substance in the body that the alchemists termed "The Elixir of Life."[123] At transitions, the timelessness of the soul enters the body. In me it created the keloid. It connected me to the personal and the transpersonal, to the past, the present and the future simultaneously. Scars are held sacred by those who endure the pain of their intentional creation. For me, they appeared like stigmata upon my body in moments of extreme psychological pain. My life circled around this central point where the eternal touched the body and manifested as scars.

The death and rebirth motif, personal and collective identification, and the need for protection and for a living relationship to the spirits in the hereafter were all part of ritual ceremonial scarification. By incising themselves and producing scars, the initiates connected to their clan-ancestors, representatives of the collective unconscious. Active imagination with the scars was my form of divination, an attempt to consult their voice as a guide. Subsequent active imaginations brought new insights and images that embellished the theme of the scars' evolution. Two active imaginations were poignant. The first suggested: "With the raw closeness of death around my newborn self, pieces of the afterworld got into me and reemerged in the form of the keloid scar." The second active imagination included the following: "I was burned by the fires of crossing from another world into this one, and the keloids marked the event. They continued to mark each subsequent crossing."

In traditional cultures body art provides protection from evil spirits to which people are particularly vulnerable at the time of their initiations. The initiate "seeks to display his allegiance to that which is signified by the mark . . . . the sign is expected to 'reciprocate' this display of sacrifice"[124] and thus provide protection. Carrying a symbol on one's skin encourages the person to stay connected with her/his archaic roots in the instinctual layer of the psyche where the symbolic images reside. Integrating the symbols into one's total personality offers continued protection when they are consciously taken up by the individual who contemplates their meaning.

The scars came to me as a natural protection from "evil spirits" (i.e., a fear of death attending new development) and returned at each subsequent initiation. In addition, the psychological work inspired *by* the scars brings increasing consciousness. Consciousness is itself a protection. If scarification prevents the invasion of the evil spirits, then to live out what scarification means continues to actively ward off the evil spirits. One must participate consciously with the body's powers of healing, along with the purposeful sacrifices required to usher in the new development.

My own scars protected me from succumbing psychologically to the potentially disabling effects of my birth and childhood. I would have been far more disturbed had they not carried the chaotic residue my psyche was left to deal with. By deflecting the evil spirits, they defended against the returning chaos that threatened to pull me under. The scars spoke for me. As I realized this, I began to see that I must shift from having the scars protect me to taking up the task myself.

Traditional initiation ceremonies are held to permit a person to leave the parental bond and join the larger cultural group. The giving and receiving of an enduring mark represents the death of the old and the birth of new life. The cut of the knife and the resulting pain make real a separation from the old familial connections and ensure that the initiate feels a new identity. My own scars let me reach beyond the mother and separate from the personal part of the relationship. As well, by reflecting my wounded aspects, the scars would ultimately become the vital source of my transformation.

I have valued the spontaneous scars as the object upon which I projected the opposites within my psyche: the lower aspects (feeling abandoned and inferior) and the higher aspects (the spiritual side of the psyche that came alive for me by investigating the meaning of the scars themselves). What I projected on the scar (i.e., what the scar means to me) is similar to what indigenous people project on it — namely, the scar represents and carries messages from the spirit world, reminders of initiations and passages, victories and defeats, new life and death. The scars are vestiges of what was once encountered and is now left behind.

As part of my exploration I began to contemplate the relevance of this material to the modern day rage for body piercing and tattooing, which has been called "modern primitivism."[125] Analysts observing this phenomenon have noted: "Amidst an almost universal feeling of powerlessness to 'change the world,' individuals are changing what they have power over: their own bodies . . . . By giving visible expression to unknown desires and latent obsessions welling up from within, individuals can provoke change."[126] In *The Body*, George Elder also observed: "[T]attoos are images of the deepest reaches of the human psyche, images with which one's ego is brought into relationship, for the sake of the necessary feeling that one's individual identity is meaningful and the feeling that one is deeply connected to the group."[127]

For indigenous people, the most commonly held belief regarding scarification and tattooing is that they are preventive. The highly visible scars produce a disconnection from a hurtful spirit source. This may also apply today. "One of the most important impulses behind tattooing seems to be a search for identity in a precarious situation."[128] Understood psychologically, they are a protective buffer from the darkness outside — from the unknown that faces one in times of change and from the darkness within — from affects and emotions that threaten to overwhelm the ego. Without a meaningful ritual for the psyche to contain these primitive urges, the unconscious can break through.

In the last decade of the twentieth century, the psyche was beginning to seek some way to express the numinous. Contemporary body marking seems to express this longing for spiritual initiation as a counterbalance to the chaos of the undifferentiated psyche at times of great change. It is my view that marking the body reflects the desired conjunction of spirit and matter and aspires to move the psyche toward a transformed, integrated state.

Although usually not at a conscious level, marking the body is an expression of the process of individuation; one sets forth on one's path and seeks a means of expressing the voice that calls from within. Body decoration is one such means. Psychologically, a person who has an image engraved on her/his body is seeking a tangible and permanent expression of the inner voice. Expressing it in an art form brings it further into reality.

The design realized first in the unconscious and then carved on the skin has an important message to convey. When that message is realized consciously, it furthers the process of transformation. The creative force that lives in the body asks to be realized. It is divine energy and has the potential to lead the ego toward a new development, to know more about oneself, the unconscious, and the world.

I had carried the transformational aspects in my unconscious and then in my body. Later, I had contemplated and studied them, but something in me was still unrealized, incomplete. I needed to experience them in a more integrated way. On one occasion, as we were on the way to the actual hotel where my mother and I had met in my dream, a colleague told me a story that turned out to be a seed that would ultimately bring about integration. It was only years later that I realized that this colleague had many of the qualities of my mother and lived her life as my mother had. It was as if the psyche had chosen her to sit in for my mother. Our association fed the "starved lion" (the earlier dream image) inside me.

She told me about her safari in Africa, where a dramatic event left a deep impression on her. Lions had surrounded a wildebeest, isolating it for the kill. One was at its side, one pulling the tail, and one was at its neck. The others were circling around the condemned animal. As it was dying it uttered the bellows of the ultimate surrender to death. I was mesmerized by this story. The struggle of the dying animal was my struggle, and the sound echoed in me for a long time. It touched me in the place where I heard my mother's cry when part of my psyche died with her.

Shortly thereafter, I had a dream about this colleague.

> *I am in a cavern with deep water, and I am standing on a*
> *stone platform pulling out corpses that have just crossed over.*
> *The woman who had told me the story of the wildebeest*
> *is the one I am pulling out next. There is a pile of children's bodies*
> *nearby, and one child is still alive.*

This dream had an authentic feeling of what the other world would be like, just like the corpses Plato describes at the end of his long dialogue on the nature of the afterlife in "The Republic."[129] Pulling up my friend seemed to indicate my need to pull up the thread of my life's work. She represented the African story and the journey to hear the lecture when my mother came to sit behind me. This is what I needed to "pull together" for the next phase of my journey. I was standing on the stone platform, my own *prima materia*, my own stone, my own individuality, and it could now be seen in a much larger light — the light of eternity.

This dream was an image of death, but one child was yet alive; she hadn't died in the crossing. There was still time to bring her back to life. This child represented my deep interest in bringing together the two main events in my life, the scars and the death of my mother. I needed to bring them out of the unconscious and into the world while I was alive, and I had to go beyond my everyday world, which until then continued to be characterized by a fearful attitude and too-small outlook. It was time for me to apply my growing knowledge in a larger context.

# CHAPTER EIGHT

# GOING TO AFRICA

*[I]t is the self that causes me to make the sacrifice;*
*nay more, it compels me to make it.*[130]

As my interest in scarification intensified, I became fully engaged in my research. In libraries I found as much information as I could on scarification rites and pored over pictures of scarified people. I was invited by the director of a cultural history museum on a private tour to view the collections in storage. My compelling interest was being authenticated. I saw the actual artifacts I had read about and felt the essence of the eternal in my hands. That remarkable opportunity carried me for quite a while. I then was invited into a few people's homes to see their private collections. Doors began to open as my passion came to life. Soon I began to interview people who had done research in Africa: art historians, writers, anthropologists, and museum curators. When I told them about my desire to explore the links between the ritual of scarification and my own spontaneous scars, not only were they immediately receptive to me, but each one encouraged me to go to Africa to meet scarified people. An outer-world journey on a grander scale was part of this process; there was no way around it.

Whenever I thought about making such a trip — whenever I talked about it or read a book by someone who had been there, or whenever there was any mention of Africa — tears would well up in me from a totally unknown source. The tears resonated with the tale of my colleague's African safari and my identification with the wail of the wildebeest. Along with the people of Africa, that wail was calling me home. The fact that I identified with the animal that was attacked and killed meant that I, too, had been and now needed to be a sacrificial object for something greater than my everyday existence. Africa was the land where human life originated, the cradle of civilization where the scars were born and the eternal was palpable. Something in me had to be on that land, close to that sound.

I wanted to go where people bear these sacred marks and where they are the visible evidence that the body holds the buried mysteries.

The scars had been made deep within me, and going to Africa to study them was my fate, my odyssey in search of wholeness. To fulfill myself and bring my research and work into fruition I had to make this journey. I was following the keloid's passage into being. My psychological wholeness would be reflected in the union of the scars and their archetypal source, the source where the scars, my protection, had originated. Returning the keloid to its source would return me to mine.

Jung wrote about alchemist Michael Maier's mystic journey to "the intense heat of [the African] summer. He was approaching that region of the psyche . . . . from humanity's past epochs . . . [the] deepest down of all, [that dwells in man's psychology] the transcendental mystery and paradox of the sympathetic and parasympathetic psychoid processes."[131] This was where the scars had been born.

As the momentum toward a concrete journey to Africa began to grow, I had a dream of African animals trying to get into my too-small room. The elephant's trunk and the giraffe's head reached in the window to meet me. In another dream I was among a group of young African women, dancing in the night, our bodies glistening with oil, hoping to attract a mate. After these persistent dreams I began to work to bring this trip about. I made some inquiries of people who might facilitate my journey. For several years these contacts produced nothing. Then in January 1994, after meeting someone who seemed more reliable than the others and while waiting to hear from him, I awoke in the middle of the night and wrote in my journal: "If I belong to the keloid, it is like a marriage that I gladly participate in. It is the only way to continue on — connecting to the continuum — going back in time to Africa and forward in time for the sake of the life process." One week later I got the phone call that the trip was on.

During the two-month preparation period I wrote down my thoughts and feelings. These are some excerpts:

> To find my brothers and sisters inside the scars I have to
> journey to the other side of the world, the origins of
> their birth. I am bringing my spirit and my flesh to the
> ancestral spirits. The deepest part of me is written on
> the skin, hieroglyphs of the ancestors' voices, beckoning
> me to hear them there, not for my death but for their
> fulfillment in me. It is the Self wanting to express itself;

this is the fruit I must yield to and participate in. With this trip I am making my process visible. The gift of a lifetime unfolds before me.

My husband agreed to join me on the trip; the unconscious supported the journey and sent me this dream a week before we left.

> I am in Zurich taking a tour through Jung's house
> and am looking at the 'bare bones' of his furniture.
> His son gives me a key to the tower.
> I ask if it will open Jung's private room there, and he says,
> "The key will open everything."

I had wanted to see the tower Jung built at Bollingen ever since I read about it. This dream told me that going to Africa would be the equivalent. Undertaking this journey was unique to me and was the key to building my own tower. The keloids were the centuries-old stones, the bare bones of my foundation. I had entered their world, and they had entered mine. I was about to leave my old containment and descend further into their world, into a much larger piece of my totality. I was leaving the imprisonment of the old, outdated tower. That was also the key.

During the last week of preparation for the journey, I experienced the Self as if it were coming into consciousness and offering itself to me. It was giving birth to me, and I was giving birth to it. It wanted to see Africa through my eyes, and I was a welcome sacrifice for this to happen. Jung wrote about this: "We have seen that a sacrifice only takes place when we feel the self actually carrying it out on ourselves."[132] For me, going to Africa was an imperative from the Self. I was like one of the Englishmen Jung commented on, going out to posts in various African colonies: "[T]hese passengers were not traveling for pleasure, but were entering upon their destiny."[133] I was part of the rhythm of life, the unstoppable contractions that have an autonomy of their own.

By undertaking this journey, I was bridging the two sides of myself — the injured orphan child and the hero exploring the keloid. The Self had unfolded organically in presenting me with these marks. I would take up the task of its continued unfolding. Travel in the outer world had always been difficult for me, but when travel was associated with my interest in the keloid, it was an entirely different matter. If my relationship to the keloid was "like a marriage," the journey I was about to take would be the honeymoon. The trip was to be to West Africa, where I would meet the scarified people who reflected my soul.

Through a series of synchronicities I met Malidoma Somé, an elder and diviner from the Dagara people of Burkina Faso, West Africa. Several meetings I had with him before we left helped prepare me for the journey. We discussed my desire to go to the villages and maybe even see a scarification ceremony being performed. He had a friend in Africa who would be our host. I telephoned his friend in Burkina Faso shortly before we left and told him what I wanted to accomplish, but we had no precise plan other than to meet him at the airport. We were open to letting the adventure unfold.

We flew first to Paris before taking a connecting flight to Ouagadougou, the capital city of Burkina Faso, a landlocked country in the center of West Africa, formerly called Upper Volta. I was looking out of the window as we passed over the Mediterranean Sea and flew over the coastline of northern Africa. There was no stopping me now. For about four hours we passed over desert, and then suddenly, like a mirage, the city appeared, and we descended into her arms. I was coming home.

We deplaned and went through customs. I went outside to find our host so he could help us. He was standing in a crowd of people awaiting those who had arrived. Next to him was a man he had located to be our guide. He was holding up a sign with our name on it. It was a great relief to find them. I needed our host to vouch for us to the authorities so they would let us proceed, luggage intact. Our host introduced our guide as "someone who knows the countryside as opposed to someone who speaks fluent English." When we drove to the hotel a short distance away we passed a myriad of people riding bikes and motor scooters. Many of the women were dressed in colorful fabrics, walking with babies on their backs and heavy pans or jars of water on their heads. I felt very much at home. I had my assignment and a purpose to fulfill, and I was where I had always wanted to be.

During our first evening in the country, we had dinner with both our host and guide. Our host was a university professor with an American Ph.D. who knew a bit about Jung and about the collective unconscious, which I had certainly not expected. It made it much easier to explain the purpose of my visit. I said that I had spontaneous scars, that I felt I had shared ancestors with the scarified people, and that I was there to see and interview them. He translated what I said into French for our guide, who nodded his head receptively. They both seemed to resonate with the idea immediately. My husband had a good laugh over the fact that the collective unconscious is hard enough to understand in English, let alone jumping right into the heart of it within a few hours of our arrival, but they understood exactly what I was interested in. That was a good indication of what was about to unfold.

That night in the hotel, as I sat on my bed, I wrote my first entry into my journal.

> Entering Africa is like merging with an ancient soul
> who has invited me in as a guest. Something very
> deep has been waiting for me to go beyond the mother
> experience down to the very core of myself. It is as if I
> am crossing from one world to the next, as if my psy-
> che needed to do that for itself and took me along. I
> am reunited with a source from which I had long
> been separated.

The next morning when we walked outside the hotel, numerous children and adults, many crippled and begging for money, descended upon us. It was hard not to respond to each one of them. Our guide kept us focused on what needed to be done. We walked first to the bank to exchange some currency, then to the U.S. Embassy to register, and finally to the car rental agency. It was pure pleasure to walk along on those roads of red earth. It was dusty and hot, but I hardly noticed. It was beyond my wildest dreams that we were here, and it was hard to take it all in and contain my excitement. We came back for lunch and sat in the hotel's outdoor restaurant under a thatched roof, watching the cook grilling the chicken we had ordered. It all tasted wonderful.

The following day we picked up the rented car and prepared to go to various villages in the interior of the country. The hotel was our home base. We were away anywhere from a day to five days at a time. Our guide took us first to his village, a drive of about three hours, and I absorbed the landscape as we went along. The terrain was dry desert with low shrubs, acacias and baobab trees. The main road was paved, but we wove around large potholes as we passed many villages set back from the road. Most weren't visible, but occasionally we could see the outer walls on the periphery. The villages had open plazas, mud-walled buildings concentrated in compounds with either flat or conical roofs.

We were there during the hottest time of the year, 120 degrees Fahrenheit in the daytime. It was dry heat, and a hat was essential, as were sunscreen and insect repellent. Eventually we turned onto the road that led to Bagassi, our guide's village in the area inhabited by the Bwa people. We parked the car and walked into the courtyard. We sat down on a long bench they provided for us and were immediately greeted by some of the women and a few men, many with beautiful scarified faces!

Our guide asked me as we sat before the villagers, "My friend (our host) said it was many years that you have wanted to come here?" "Twenty years," I said. His question put me immediately in touch with my feelings. He had dropped to a deeper level, acknowledging the importance of my being there. The children came out from their hiding places and gathered around. They stood across from us in a group, staring and smiling. We stared and smiled back. A wave of feeling rose up in me. This was what I had come for. I felt I was one of them. (figs. 40A–B show children from two villages.)

We walked through the compound to meet the elders who were five minutes away. When one first arrives in a village, one greets the people who come out and then meets with the elders (including the chief) to tell them the reason for the visit (fig. 41). Our guide, who was the

Fig. 40A: *Children from Dogona.*

144

Fig. 40B: *An afternoon in Dossi.*

Fig. 41: *Chief from Bagassi.*

nephew of one of the elders, vouched for us with the chief. As we were walking, the children came right along with us. Wherever we walked, they wanted to hold my hand, and I loved every minute of it. I was as excited as they were, and I wanted the contact as much as they did.

We arrived at the area where the elders were sitting and sat down across from them. Our guide talked with them first in their native language, Bwamu, about his life and their own and, among other things, asked their permission for us to take photographs. Once permission was granted he photographed some of the villagers. He knew exactly what I wanted to capture, and once I relaxed, I also took pictures. No one in the village spoke English, and our guide spoke only French and very limited English. Thus we experienced the whole event in a raw and unmediated way.

We took a tour of the village. Within the compounds are open plazas with family living quarters, cattle pens where the livestock is guarded, places where the food is prepared, and an outdoor shrine to their ancestors. There was no plumbing or electricity; kerosene lamps provided light. Since it was late and we were tired from the long drive, they took us to a house they had prepared for us at the edge of the compound. It was too hot to stay inside, so we put up our mosquito net on the porch and tried to get some rest. My eyes didn't want to close. I didn't want to miss a thing.

That night I wrote in my journal:

> This is like the original family I had always known, who have come to welcome me home. Maybe this is what death is like: when you arrive all the children gather around to greet you, and the old women shake your hand and ask if you are well ("maberra, maberra"), and you meet the council of elders and they say it is o.k. to photograph. Being here makes me feel genuine. I feel a kinship with these women with scarified faces. They are here doing their work, and I am here doing mine. Here is where my soul resides among the ancestors and their living kin. It is a flower garden coming to life for me. For indigenous people, life has an inherent balance. Everything is honored for what it is. There is hierarchy and order in the village, simplicity and beauty in the people and their land, and they

146

accept what has to be done. I pray to my body to please stay strong so I can do what I have come to accomplish. We are the only white people here. I feel overwhelmed by the privilege.

When we were left on our own to sleep, we were surrounded by unfamiliar noises (the braying of the donkeys, the pigs close by us). Then a small creature crawled over me and that, along with the unknown of it all, caused both of us to stay up all night. Two men came up on the porch and prepared a place to sleep. My husband thought they were sent to protect us. It turned out that they slept there every night. I wondered what the rest of the villagers were doing at that moment. I wanted to be everywhere at once. It was all magical to me.

In the morning the children returned and came up on the porch to sit near us. One little girl stared a long time at me, shyly hiding behind a post and then coming back out again. We just smiled at one another, but I wished I could talk with her. She stayed close to me when we walked about, and I managed to take a photograph of her (fig. 42).

Fig. 42: *Little girl from Bagassi.*

The village chief came to see us, bearing a live chicken as a gift. The day before we had given the elders some gifts we had brought, and he was reciprocating. My husband had an inspiration for which I will always be grateful. He asked if they would permit us to offer the chicken as a gift to their ancestors and conduct a ritual sacrifice. Initially the elders were astounded by our request, but after a brief deliberation agreed to the ceremony.

When the people of the village make a sacrifice it is a highly sacred event. For the Africans, sacrificing an animal, a precious commodity there, is a way of connecting to the ancestors. Through sacrifice they thank the ancestors for what they have been given, and they request blessings for the future. The elders assembled with the shaman of the village and sat in a circle; we sat nearby (figs. 43–48). They said the initial prayers and proceeded through the stages of the sacrifice ceremony, which is a form of divination. After the chicken is killed and defeathered, they examine the entrails to see if they are clean. If they are, and it is not always the case, it means the ancestors have accepted the sacrifice. In our case, the entrails were clean. To me this meant that the divine authorities had accepted my life's efforts and let this be known and witnessed in a public setting.

Fig. 43: *Chicken sacrifice in Bagassi. The elders assembled with the shaman-priest and sat in a circle.*

Figs. 44-46: *The chicken is killed and defeathered.*

Fig. 45

Fig. 46

Fig. 47: *The entrails of our chicken were clean.*

Fig. 48: *Celebration after the ceremony.*

When a member of the village returns after some period of being away, a sacrifice is performed in his or her honor. Our chicken sacrifice was to me the celebration of my homecoming. The elders and a few others who had gathered were especially pleased because, as we were told later, they took a risk in offering to do a sacrifice for us and possibly offending the ancestors. We were the first white people ever to make a sacrifice in that village. Heaven opened up a little more.

After the ceremony, the elders told us that the ancestors would provide continuing protection for the duration of our stay in Africa and that we would be coming back to the village. Though we hadn't planned to do so, we did in fact return before we left Africa. A friend of our guide, whom he asked to accompany us as a second guide, said to us in utter sincerity, "You will be protected because of your sacrifice." And he was right. During the subsequent three weeks of the trip, in third world conditions with many diseases, extreme heat and unfamiliar food, we managed to stay well. The chicken sacrifice was an auspicious beginning for our stay in Africa; we felt we were truly initiated into African life. To this day I am convinced that the Africa trip came about because I had written, "I belong to the keloid."

I had concentrated my work on the keloid, and it reciprocated by showing me its people and its ceremonies. The ancestors had approved and invited me home.

A few days after our ceremony we were privileged to go to Dafra, a place of worship where an individual or a family can make sacrifices. It is a sacred place with a waterfall whose source is unknown. Below is a pool of water containing sacred large freshwater fish (similar to koi). When we were there, two men and a woman arrived. The man was carrying a goat around his neck. The other two carried a chicken and a pigeon. They went up to a small ledge near us and made a sacrifice, saying their prayers. We stood in silence and watched the whole thing from a short distance away. The man cut the jugular vein of the goat and bled it. Then he laid the goat on the rocks, and they said more prayers. We walked by the goat and stood before it a long time, looking at it as it lay dying, looking up at us. Our journey was divinely inspired, and events occurred in a totally unexpected way. Not only had the chicken sacrifice been performed in our honor, but now we were watching a private sacrifice ceremony. These were important spiritual moments from another culture. It was like being in the biblical temple when animal sacrifices were made.

Several days later our guide took us to his mother's village so I could meet her and see the elaborate scarification on her back. From there we drove to a village called Tiébélé (fig. 49). Here the symbols of the psyche are carved not only on the body but on the houses and on sculptures

Fig. 49: *Designs carved on the structures in Tiébélé.*

and pottery. The designs are the communication between human beings and spirits.

Burkina Faso is one of the poorest countries in the world, but it has great cultural wealth. We observed this in two mask ceremonies. Wooden masks represent either animals or abstract designs. The designs carved on the masks parallel the scars made on faces and bodies and are always symbolic of a larger dimension. The mask lets the spirit connect to people. The mask wearer is entirely overtaken by spirit. During performances, the mask wearer changes internally as well as in appearance. He is possessed by the spirit he is incarnating.

In the village of Yarmako we saw a dance celebrating one of these masks (fig. 50). Many dignitaries came to this performance, which was dedicated to the fertility of the land. People sought a blessing for their

Fig. 50: *Mask dedicated to farming in Yarmako.*

crops and sometimes advice as to where the crops should be planted. The mask is seen only every seventeen years, only three times in a local person's lifetime. And we happened to be there.

The *griot* (one of a hereditary group of musicians, storytellers and performers of ceremonies) wears the mask. *Griots* go through many initiations. They are considered sacred people and can't eat from the communal pot; they are very socially restricted. The *griot* goes into the bush the night before a ceremony and communes with the ancestors. The plant fibers for the mask are gathered during the night. The fibers embody supernatural forces that act on behalf of the clan. Some masks are constructed of plaited, dyed wood and decorated with geometric designs on the head crests. The masks act as emissaries of man, while still remaining entities of the bush. An artful synthesis of the two worlds, they are regarded as the perfect conciliators in all spiritual matters.

The mask wearer holds two knives representing the process of sacrifice. Hitting the two knives together represents male and female generating life. Each dance step the *griot* makes has a symbolic meaning. Music and people are always around the mask. I was told by the man who invited us that this mask is supposed to be very fast, faster than a normal man walking. He said, "Sometimes he goes from village to village. A normal man will do it in an hour, and this mask is supposed to do it in less than twenty minutes. He's on the wings of the wind. My grandfather said he put his hand on his back, and he got such a burn."[134]

At the communal celebration, before the mask makes its appearance, the village women dance with rhythmic steps in a large circle. We sat among the dignitaries and watched them. After the mask appeared, the dignitaries gathered for a meal, and we met the President of the Burkina Parliament. He asked, though an interpreter, what I did for a living. I was honored that he took an interest in my presence there.

We were also privileged to attend a funeral ceremony. A friend of our guide's was preparing a funeral for his father, who was the former chief of the village. The son told us his father was the most respected elder in the village and had fought with General DeGaulle against the Germans when the country was called Upper Volta. He was clearly highly respected in the area as hundreds turned out for the ceremonies, including the chief of the village and the government representative in the area. The mask that came out for the funeral was the oldest mask of the village of Karaba (fig. 51). It represented a female panther, a blend of strength and tolerance. There are special drums that are saved only for occasions involving this particular mask.

The night before the mask arrived, the chief of the village spoke to a gathering of villagers and guests through a *griot*, who stood in front of a crowd seated in a circle. The chief didn't speak in a formal way directly to the villagers but only through an intermediary who shouted and chanted the chief's words. Many of the villagers stayed up all night, performing more ceremonies in preparation for the funeral. We didn't join them during that time, because we wanted to be fresh and awake in the morning to see the mask. The next day we sat with the family while we waited for the mask to appear. We were the only white people there, but we felt we were part of the landscape, the festivities, and their village family.

The mask that came out for the funeral was the most important mask, the first mask of the village. The *griots* decide when this mask will come out, whether the occasion warrants it. The mask performed a series of dances at several locations in the village. A few people danced along with the *griot*. After the mask dance we joined the son's

Fig. 51: *Funeral mask in Karaba.*

family for dinner. They cooked chicken and rice for us as they knew what food we could eat.

Both of the mask dances we attended revealed just how synchronistic our visit was with the people and their sacred rituals. We were told that the day before we arrived, the sheep that the son had bought to be used for the funeral sacrifice had been stolen and that he was totally broke and despondent. He had gone to the bar at the nearby cotton factory, where we met him for the first time. Knowing nothing of this, and after visiting his father's shrine at his invitation, we gave him some money as a contribution to the festivities. That money paid for another sheep, and he was able to replace the original one without anyone knowing it had been stolen by a thief from outside the village. He didn't feel it was a coincidence, especially because he wasn't expecting us to be there. He said to me that perhaps he and I were brother and sister in another lifetime. We also learned later that we were the only people the son took into the family shrine. His step-brother asked him why he took two white people "totally different than anybody here" into the shrine when he didn't take anyone else. He later told me that he had communicated with his dead father, who gave his son permission to let us in because he and I were related.

When we were talking the day before the funeral I told the son and his mother that the main purpose of my being in Africa was to see scar-ification. The mother, the chief's wife, told me of her scarification, done for cosmetic reasons when she was young. We went off to talk alone. I showed her my scars, and she showed me hers. This was further evi-dence that the journey was divinely inspired, as these events occurred in a totally unexpected manner. In many ways, the trip was a living active imagination, because the spiritual aspect was omnipresent. It confirmed the Self's design in this whole, amazing journey. I had sacri-ficed my fear and my reluctance to enter into life when I undertook the trip, and the Self seemed to be responding in a most favorable way. I had concentrated my work on the keloids' origins, and it was recipro-cating by showing me its people and its ceremonies.

When we went to Bobo Dioulasso, our guide called on a friend who taught English in the high school there. His friend arranged several interviews with healers in the area and accompanied us on our out-ings. He was quite warm, attentive and acutely sensitive to our needs and my purpose in being there. When I voiced my concern about what we would do if the car broke down and we were stranded in the heat in the middle of "nowhere," he said, "Don't even picture it. Don't even think about it." He was the man I mentioned earlier who, when we would worry, would say in utter sincerity, "You will be protected because of your sacrifice." And he was right.

One of the activities he and our guide suggested was a visit to see some hippopotami in a remote lake outside of town. When we arrived and looked out at this tranquil lake I was captivated. Our guide and his friend, along with my husband and myself, sat in a wooden canoe as the boatman stood in back, rowing us gently along, until we came as close to the hippos as we could safely get. We sat a while and watched them, their heads just above the water keeping an eye on us as we were looking at them. In this serene setting, with gorgeous flowering vegetation on the water and only one other boat with two fishermen in sight, I kept thinking that if people knew about this idyllic, picturesque scene they would come here in droves. When we got back to shore, we were greeted by a group of villagers who had gathered while we were out, watching over us I imagined, like incarnations of the ancestors who were undoubtedly with us during our sojourns.

When we dined with our host I would discuss with him my increasing understanding of my purpose in making this journey. Several times he said how glad they were to be a part of it. It was heartwarming to have him say that, and he obviously meant it, indicating that my presence and my research gave them something as well. We didn't attend an initiation ceremony, but our host showed us a video he had made of a group of young men returning to his own village after their initiation. He told us that for three months the initiates stay in the bush and learn about their tribe and their new responsibilities in becoming men. During the initiation they get new names, as if they were in the womb. In those three months they learn about sexuality, learn a secret language, and make their masks.

The video showed the week-long ceremony that takes place when the initiates return to the village wearing their costumes. At the conclusion, they take off their masks. Flute playing always accompanies them, and they dance in a circle, stepping in a particular rhythm. People from neighboring villages gather for the coming-home ceremony. Our host also told us that each person has a kinship with an animal, like an antelope or a lion or turtle, and when that person dies, people with the same animal identity bring their masks to the funeral.

On another evening our host joined us on the patio of the hotel in

Bobo Dioulasso (the second largest city in the country) and told us some stories. One was about his being treated for a scorpion bite. The traditional remedy was to push the venom down the leg away from the heart and out the site. When the remedy was applied to him it didn't work. The healer told him that something had happened to someone close to him. Later he found out that at that moment, his best friend had died. In further discussion, he told us, "The African way is indirect and roundabout, not linear, direct or immediate. If you pushed for an answer too quickly you would be told another story — like a story about an impatient bird that died. This would be a warning not to press too quickly for answers."

He talked about the spiritual life of the village and how much happier they are than people in the cities. There is a sense of the collective in the village. People don't ask, "How are you?" but rather, "How is your family?" The village environment is very supportive, and no one starves for want of food there. But that isn't true in the cities, where many people struggle to get enough food or water to drink, a problem that was made worse by the devaluation of the local currency in the 1990's.

When we stopped back in our guide's village before we left, it was exhilarating to see familiar faces again. Just as I was admiring an old woman's skirt, our guide's aunt, having first received his permission, invited me into a hut where other women had gathered. They presented me with a piece of fabric as a gift. It was just like the woman's skirt, embroidered figures on lined cotton cloth. I was utterly astonished, and I held onto that piece of fabric until we arrived back at our hotel. I wasn't about to let it out of my sight, and I knew just where I would put it in our home — on the wall in the living room where it would be one of the first things people saw after coming in the front door.

The elders wished us a safe journey back to the States, and we made the long trip back to our hotel in silence. When we arrived and walked through the cocktail area there was music playing, as was the case each evening. Those melodies will always be with me. The music conveyed the grace we were experiencing. As an offering of thanksgiving, I buried a lock of my hair in the ground nearby, so that a part of me would always be there, integrated in that earth forever.

One of the most touching and personally meaningful connections happened on our last day in Africa, when our guide happened to ask a young woman along the road (whom he knew from his village) if she could direct us to get change for the road tax. When she came up to the car I noticed she had scars on her arm *exactly* like my scars. She also had a large keloid on her face. I could hardly contain myself and asked her if we could go off alone together. She showed me the scars on her back and her chest, and I showed her mine. When I told her I wanted to take her picture she went to get her baby (fig. 52).

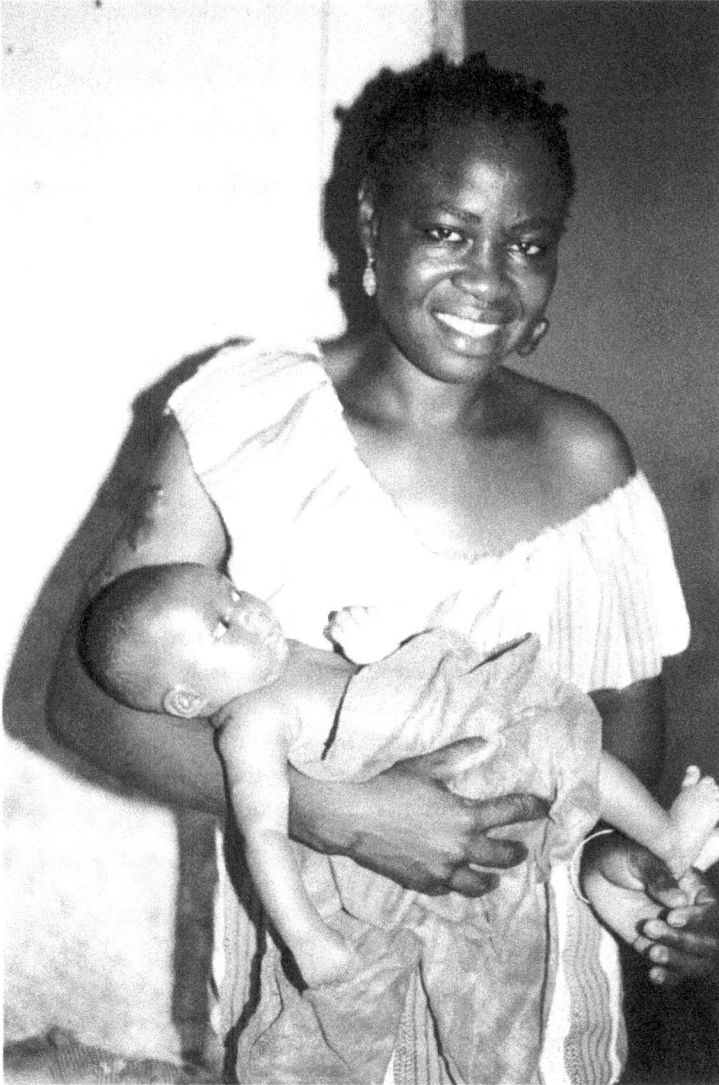

Fig. 52: *Woman with keloids.*

Finding her was like finding "the jewel that is discovered in the most common place." She came as if from nowhere at the end of our journey. After seeing many beautiful scarifications on the villagers and in the cities — from the gas station attendants to the dignitaries at the ceremonies — I found her. She was a mirror image of myself, a stranger on the road, a "soul sister" who seemed to have waited for me to accomplish what I had come for so that we could meet. Scarred and scarified, the two merged as one.

When I was in Africa I was a guest and yet one of the people at the same time. I had never forgotten them entirely. It seemed as if I had sprung from this place, and my spirit had never left. In Africa I was descending into the heart of the scar and into the heart of myself. I continued to write in my journal.

> In Africa I am finally with the scarified people of my ancient soul. People accept this quest of mine and open themselves to me. The people here partake of the ancestor spirits and conduct rituals that pass between one world and another. By undertaking this journey I am participating in that passage. This is where I can be myself. In reconstructing the journey of the keloid through time, I am reconstructing the journey of my own soul. To enter the black land as the white envoy on behalf of the keloid is to integrate the soul of the keloid and the soul of the motherland into my soul. Africa is a view into eternity. It is like the cave for me, and I am privileged to be here as its guest. God had carved out a space for me to integrate my suffering and begin anew. My tears preceding the trip were in anticipation of the initiation that is under way. In this "natural world" my "natural" mother lives.

# CHAPTER NINE

# THE SHAMANS' MESSAGE

*The spirit dwells in what is not attractive to human eyes. It is an invitation for a modification of the psyche in order to appreciate the hidden beauty behind it.*[135]

I interviewed five local shamans while we were in Africa (two are pictured in figs. 53–54). Interpreters translated from their native language into French and then into English. I wasn't able to go into much depth, but the experience of talking with them turned out to be more valuable than the content. It was like speaking directly to ancient souls. The wisdom of the ancestors came through the shamans' words, peeling away deeper layers of the keloid's mystery. I wrote: "The shamans speak to me. This is my initiation. Since the mother did not convey her wisdom directly, this is doubly important for me."

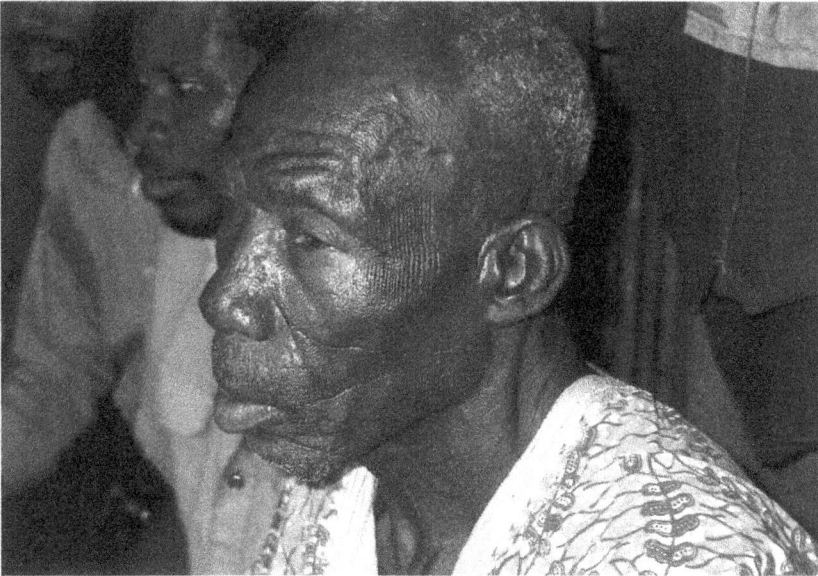

Fig. 53: *Shaman from Dossi.*

Fig. 54: *Bobo elders from Dioulassoba.*

After the chicken sacrifice in Bagassi, I had my first interview with a shaman in a nearby village. When we arrived, the shaman, as is customary, asked why we wanted to talk with him. When my interest in scarification was made known to him, the shaman asked us to move from the porch where he was sitting into his hut. The shaman's powers are secret, and he apparently didn't want to talk about them in front of his people.

I addressed my questions to our guide, who spoke a little English; he translated into French and his cousin then translated into the local language of Bwamu for the shaman. During our interview, a group of young children gathered outside the doorway to his hut. One little girl was crying inconsolably. She may have been forlorn without her mother, or she may never have seen white people before and was afraid. With utmost compassion, the healer went to the door and tenderly picked her up, brought her inside and wrapped the long fabric of his clothing around her as she sat at his feet. It calmed her down immediately. She stayed with us for the remainder of the time.

This first healer arranged for me to interview a facial scarifier who lived nearby. Initially this particular healer was reluctant to talk to me because of his previous experience with people from the government.

Since facial scarification was officially forbidden, he was naturally guarded. But the older healer with whom I had been talking encouraged him to speak freely to me, and so he did. When I asked him about scarification in relationship to a death, he responded, "According to certain beliefs we scar a child who dies right after his birth so that the mother, when she has another child — we say it's the same child who comes back — in order that she does not hurt too much. We especially scar to show this child to the evil spirit which is in him — that we recognized him (the evil spirit) so that he is scarred and will not cause the death again or [that he will not] come back. The second reason to scarify is to redeem the death. In that case we scar the child to communicate with the ancestors, so that they won't let the child die again."

Subsequent interviews took place in different villages, but they followed the same protocol. At the beginning of each interview, I said that I wanted to know more about the meaning of scarification and explained to the healers that I had spontaneous scars and I felt a commonality with them because of it. This assured them I wasn't an anthropologist who had come to study them, and it allowed them to be more receptive to me and willing to tell me some of their secrets. I went on to say that I thought we had shared ancestors who had created my scars and thus created my link to them. Because of the personal nature of my quest and my psychological attitude, which resonated with their spiritual attitude, the healers spoke openly with me. The meaning behind their rituals did indeed reveal our common ground.

The interviews centered on the three main reasons that scarification is performed: ethnic identification, initiation, and healing. Scars made for initiation were mostly hidden from view, as were the ceremonies. These marks are sacred to the initiates, and the scarified people fear that if the scars are seen by someone who doesn't have a respectful attitude, the meaning and intention of the scars can be taken away. The sacred must be veiled. (I wondered if that was an underlying reason I had been so reluctant to show my own scars.) Scarification for initiation and for identification is now illegal for health reasons and because the government wishes to encourage national unity and discourage individual ethnic group identification. The healer from the Bobo people explained that scarification lasted because his ancestors didn't have any identification papers. We were also told by an elder that the young people don't want scarification on their faces because they get ridiculed at school about it. This is an example of how modernity undercuts tradition.

In an interview with a professor at the country's only university, the University of Ouagadougou, I was told mainly about scars that protected people from being sold into slavery in colonial times. He said that anyone who took a tribesperson with these scars risked automatic retaliation by the tribe. The group would fight to take him back. At the same time masters of the slave ships were averse to purchasing someone with marks, because relatives could easily identify them. He also said that slaves with facial scarification brought lower prices when they were purchased.

Scarification for healing is currently well respected and still within the law in Burkina Faso. When modern medicine cannot cure a disease, people often go to the village healers. If the healer's diagnosis suggests that the patient would benefit from scarification, such as chest infections, the healer puts a series of small cuts in the skin (generally three are made) and applies medicine directly into the wound (see fig. 35). The shaman said that sometimes the appropriate medicine appears to him in a dream.

Scarification is not only for healing physical ailments but includes psychological distress as well. I learned that scarification is performed when a person has a particular mission to accomplish but is being interfered with by a certain spirit. One woman told me her story:

> When I was still a child . . . and I would be walking, sometime I couldn't go forward. I would go backward, and I started to have convulsions. Later on as I tried to run I found myself falling. I was always on the ground. Finally I was taken to a healer or a diviner to find out what was happening, and he said that there were spirits trying to hold me from moving on. It was not just on the walking level; it was going to be for the rest of my life. It was going to stop me from carrying on my mission in life. At first what they did was to start a ritual where they tied something on my ankle just to hold me on to this side before they started to do the scarification. After that I could run without any problem and never got these kind of convulsions again.

One interview stood out from all the rest. It was the only interview I had with a woman healer. When we walked into the village to see her, it was like finding the alchemical "gold in the dung heap," for garbage was strewn all about the outskirts of the village. We walked through it to get to her, and there she was, sitting quietly in the clearing. I sat by her side (fig. 55). We did not speak directly. Through a guide, who translated for me, my questions were addressed to a man sitting across from her, who then translated to her. The healer talked about the children who were present (see fig. 35). She said, "When someone has respiratory problems and has a fever, you first have to feel his chest and know whether or not it's the right treatment. We make some little cuts around her chest. Black blood comes out of it. Then we mix the medicine powder with a small knife and put it on the wounds. It can happen that the same person goes through this treatment four or five times. There is no age for this disease. It can strike anyone, children or older people alike. All the children you see here have followed that treatment."

The Bobo healer had also talked about treating children who have respiratory problems. "We do six scars on the chest, three on the right

Fig. 55: *Woman healer from Dogona.*

165

and three on the left. The bad blood of a black color runs out, and then we rub a medicinal powder on top of it. Then we give the patient a treatment made of roots and plants that we boil together for him to drink or wash himself with. Most of the Bobo have scars on the chest, because it's a disease that's very common with children."

She was the only one to show me the charred bamboo that she used to rub into the cuts in the skin and to introduce us to some of the children she was treating. She said that if she felt the sickness wouldn't be cured by her treatment, she didn't do it. When I asked if people from other villages come to her, she said, "Yes, even the one who is your interpreter comes here to get healed." (We hadn't known that.)

When I asked the woman healer about herself, she said she was the only woman healer in the area. She also said that she inherited the powers from her mother at the age of eight, but the translator said, "She isn't sure of her age because she doesn't know when she was born because there were no records kept."

Although we did not look directly at each other, there was a palpable feeling of connection between us. I felt she was experiencing the same intensity I was feeling. It was as if we were two women who had crossed the boundaries of the everyday world and, in that moment, were experiencing together a changed time and space.

When I returned to the U.S. I continued my discussions with Malidoma Somé. My conversations with him dropped to ever-deeper levels about the meanings of scarification and my personal experience with the scars. His psychological and spiritual orientation enhanced my own understanding of the transpersonal dimension of the keloid and clarified its importance in my life. My comments, questions and reflections are interspersed in what follows.

Malidoma began his explanation of scarification with this:

> Anything that is written on the body is a hieroglyph
> that is hiding a meaning far beyond the occasion of
> its occurring. It's not accidental. Scarification serves
> the function of protecting a person from a hurtful
> spirit source. People want to deal with the problem
> before it happens.

He also said:

> Whatever shift the body undergoes can have the
> power to dissipate the current death threat. This gives
> the person strength to prepare for future battle.

This authenticated my long-held beliefs that I was meant to have the scars, for my own scars appeared at times of the greatest threat to my life energy. The initial vaccination was a signal to the ancestors, who were supporting me from afar, to come to my rescue and protect me from the dark spirits. They continued to appear whenever I needed them. The keloids defended me, as the image of the crucifix did the medieval hermits, who held it up to ward off the demons of darkness. When the scars were removed an alarm rang out for the protective forces to come back. When I told Malidoma about the Indian women of my dream and their support of me, he remarked:

> It is a dispensation to be protected, and the person is
> subject to attention on the part of evil because of it. If
> one is protected she is under close scrutiny by evil
> forces.

This confirmed that my scars reflected my continuing need to hide from death's return and to distract my orphan complexes from over-whelming my ego.

With the spontaneous scar in mind, I asked about the keloid that grows out of control during scarification. He said:

> The scar is the spirit's way to communicate — how
> the spirit explains itself to the community through the
> person. If one is being irretrievably cut and the aim is
> supposed to be healing, or if it is defined aesthetically
> in a certain predicted manner and it becomes totally
> different from what is predicted, it means the spirit
> has intervened. What people thought was in control
> is out of control. It is marked by spirit.

I asked him to say more about why the body is ritually involved on most occasions in the lives of indigenous people. His reply was:

> The body is the hotel room of the soul . . . if the body
> scar is not involved the scar done to the soul can be
> lethal to life. It can kill you.

He talked about the relationship of body and soul in regard to healing:

> The philosophy around healing and ritual is based on
> creating unanimity between body and soul. When the
> psyche undergoes trauma there's a need to quickly
> match the body's scar to the psyche's scar. Otherwise
> you find your psyche living over there and the body
> here. That is what is called a 'disembodied soul.'
> Purposefully made scars are human imitations of
> what the spirit already does. The scar makes a harmo-
> nious blend of spirit and matter.

I had felt that my own soul, blackened by death, wanted to return to
me for transformation. I told him my dream of the keloids turning into
flowers following the healing prayer, and that I wondered if the spiritual experience was aligning the soul with the body. He said in response:

> You had gone through something, and as a result there
> was this kind of stamp being gradually applied to your
> body in order to match it . . . it was an alignment of the
> body to something the soul had already undergone.

I learned from Malidoma that every time there is trauma, one either
has to learn to understand what it means . . . (in his words "the particular world he's been open to") . . . or to "cloak himself from this
world." A scar is a permanent seal affecting long-term understanding.
If one develops more syndromes or illnesses as he goes along, he gets
other scars.

Malidoma also talked about scarification and initiation:

> There's no way you can move in and out of an initia-
> tory experience with your body not having heard
> anything about it. When you get out of that, what is
> left over on your body becomes the seal that certifies
> your having gone through the process.

I talked to him about my early humiliation at having disfiguring scars, before I understood the concept and meaning of the scars as symbols of transformation. He told me that seeing the scars as a deformity was quite contrary to the understanding of them in Africa. He spoke of the attitudes of the African people toward the deformed person:

> Deformity is usually seen as a sign of great prosperity. A deformed person brings tremendous luck into his family. It's not uncommon to hear that a man who married a deformed woman or a woman who married a deformed man is marrying prosperity. A tremendous blessing is coming. The ordinary person in modern culture is repelled by deformity, seeing it as an unfortunate blow to aesthetics. The indigenous approach sees it as a window into the other world.

I talked about my artwork with the scars. He said:

> There is a relationship between your scars and your doing art. Every time you put up an image somewhere, or scribble on a blank paper, you put scars on it. The meaning is synonymous with scarification. People who wear scars need to scarify their environment to create harmonic vibration. You can't live in a sterile place. It has to be altered in some sense to have the body feel comfortable. When the body is a temple of the spirit you turn places into the temple you live in. One needs to externalize what is carried deep within . . . the eye needs to see it exteriorly.

> The symbolic movement in art is a ritual echoing what spirit is doing around you and with you. Your thoughts become the intensity of the other world, intuiting consciously that the sacredness in art is a potent way of sending your message to the other world. Something has to have the intensity to lead you, and you will become a conduit. It is a translation of your relationship with spirit and your appreciating what spirit expects of you.

Invoking the symbolic has the power to protect.
Something else is telling one what is going on, as if
hearing from one's ancient ancestors. Another layer
of messaging gives an added dimension and brings
the psyche a unification. Linking the outer and inner
moment gives a sense of completeness. The mystery
in the psyche is kept alive.

I brought my thoughts about writing, sculpting and painting into the
context of what I now understood about the spirit world. The spirit
reconfigures the body. To release the spirit, one must go to the point
where it meets the body (where it incubates in man) and decipher its
message. The investigation welcomes the spirit, accepts it, and seeks
its wisdom; that is the real partnership. When the spirit wants further
integration, making art meets it more than half way. Writing about the
symptom releases the spirit. Creating a space for symbols (in artwork
and, in this case, symbols on the skin) is a cry for the materialization
of the psyche through the incarnation of an image. Artwork centering
on the body expresses the movement in the psyche and furthers the
process of transformation. Considering one's own symptom with as
much objectivity as possible can reunite the opposites within oneself
and reinstate one's original condition of wholeness.

As for active imagination with the scars, he said:

The scars speak to you as they expect you to speak to
them. The wound is an alive thing: the divine dimension going both ways. It makes for a sacred encounter.
It is a constant going and coming to ferry their words
across to this world. When it is ritualistic there is
something healing about it. It is a birthing process
with a life of its own. The interactive work [of active
imagination] equals the kind of language spirits are
fluent in. The spirit world extends itself. They gave
you signs of that by engraving it on your body.

I began to appreciate how much I was indebted to the unconscious
and how an ongoing, reciprocal relationship to it was critical for my life
and my well-being. The way back to the inner village is through sacrifice — requesting a reconnection to it as the villagers do in performing

sacrifices to the ancestors. I engage in a private sacrifice ceremony when I approach the unconscious to ask for its wisdom and to thank it for its continuing support. Every time I fall into a complex, I need to return to the inner village and connect with my ancestors who live there.

Malidoma's message mirrored the light of the jewel, which shone all the brighter when it was reflected in these words. He spoke about the experience of the orphan, being born from the world of matter and the world of spirit, from two worlds and entering two worlds. One has to cloak oneself to disappear from the spirit world from which he/she came.

> This is what gave birth to healing being associated
> with scars. The way you do that is to change your
> configuration. Every time there is part of the healed
> body that still shows the scar, it is a constant reminder,
> like a sealing that is permanent. Never again will that
> world reach you.

I told him about my mother's death at my birth. Carrying the same name as my mother, I felt I was replacing her and that the scars were a symbolic mark of our connection. His reply and extended commentary were heartwarming:

> Souls are linked to one another by countless wires.
> They are so intimately entangled it is a radical thing to
> separate them. When a woman dies at childbirth she is
> so intricately entwined with the child it takes a miracle
> for that child to survive more than four or five years.
> There are countless experiences of this in the tribe. In
> the village there are huge ritual practices to save the
> life of the baby. Two thirds to ninety percent of the
> time the baby's soul is still with the mother on the
> other side. It takes deliberate work to bring the baby
> back. The incoming child is considered not here but
> 'adrift in a foreign world' and may leave at any time.
> Consciousness is in the other world the first year.

Then he began speaking directly to my personal situation, but it is relevant to all orphans whose mothers died or left:

You stand at the doorway between worlds. Your fascination leaves you peeking in, scrutinizing your mother's world. You were ejected from her world into this
world. The force that did that is in the other world.
You barely got into this one. She's locked in there, and
you are here. You want news from over there. The
newborn looks restlessly toward death and looks forward to her personal mother — and she doesn't have
a body anymore. Your whole life has been overcast
with this one event. It was as if you were living in
punishment and fear for your life, undeserving of its
rewards. It takes a while for a shift in consciousness to
see that the mother's life disappeared. If you are not
prepared, you translate it into guilt, that you had
something to do with it. It is energetically enervating.
If accused, you ask, "How did I do that? I don't
remember. How could I be a murderer at birth?" The
fear is that if you open your voice someone will say
you are responsible for [the death], so you shut down
your own voice once again. The guilt translates into
feeling you are dark and bad and have to keep yourself under tight check, borrowing someone else's
voice. You carry the burden of being labeled as the
cause of death. It leaves you with the tendency to
spend your whole life to make one point and the compulsion to be on the right side of people's perception.

What Malidoma said explained my pull toward my mother's world
as opposed to this one, and it described other significant elements of
my orphan psychology. These interviews reminded me of the kind
doctor of my childhood, who cared most about the effect of scars on
my psyche, and how healing that had been. Moreover, he confirmed
my hypothesis that there was a transpersonal link between my mother
and the scars. He said:

There was a merger of your mother and you, and
then the spirits become your mother. What else
would express that but the scars? Any merger involving beings from this world and another has to be

expressed in a way that is indelible. It is like a marriage ring, only bonding of this type cannot be
removed. It is the ultimate sign of oneness. Blood
spilled binds those together. Every time a scar develops, whether physically or symbolically, blood has
been spilled . . . blood being shared translates the
deep relationship with the mother who is not in this
world anymore. It is sacred. To be marked means to
know death, the death of innocence. To know death
means to be marked. The mark opens you to the
spirit world, and the door never closes.

When a life experience involves death, the scar is huge.
There is no absolution to it. The ramification of that
creates an almost sacrificial aspect to it. You would
have to sacrifice yourself to prove deep down you are
good . . . that you didn't mean harm. When caught in
the compulsion you are made to experience what your
mother experienced.

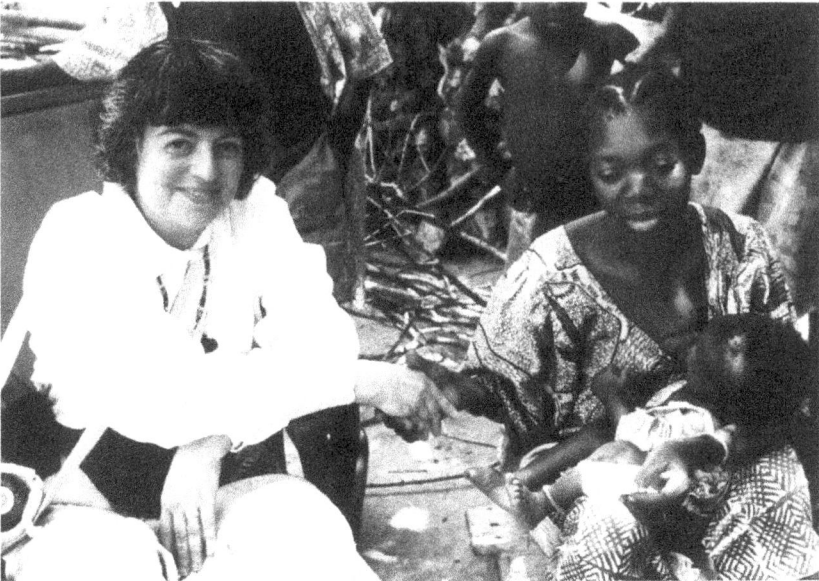

Fig. 56: *Shaking hands with the woman healer.*

This explained my sacrificial stance. My identification with my mother was strong, and I needed to become more conscious of the elements of it. When I did the painting of my mother and me, the psyche may have intended that I become conscious of this identification. Going to Africa turned out to be one way to resolve it. I had wanted to make my mother visible, as she had made herself visible to me. When I studied the photograph of myself shaking hands with the woman healer together with my painting of bringing my mother into this realm (as if holding hands) I saw they had a striking similarity (fig. 56 and fig. 27). At the deepest level this is what the journey was about. I had to experience the mother in the "motherland" of Africa and in the context of "what was higher" — my keloid research. That was the intended meaning of "bringing her across," bringing across the "higher" side of my psyche.

I passed over a threshold when I entered Africa. What had been hidden in the body and had become the scar opened itself to me consciously through the interviews with the shamans. The archetype of the keloid began to reveal its metaphysical origins and how it had become temporal. The scars were produced from the elements beyond time that reside inside the body. They connected me to the early time when the body was all man had to express himself. If I needed confirmation of the dramatic influence the archetype has on the body, there it was. The scarification archetype that moved people to perform these ceremonies had moved my genetic structure to scarify me.

Keloid scars have been intentionally produced for millennia, and my psyche resonated with the spiritual purposes and meanings of them held by indigenous people. The body was being modified with its own symbolic language, and my spontaneous scars were every bit as numinous as the scars were to the indigenous people. In alchemical terms, scarification is a means of bringing value to the body in its lowliness and ordinariness. Scarification produces jewels upon the skin. The raised keloids have been referred to as "beauty berries,"[136] and as my dream of the strapless gown illustrated, they are my flowers. When the lowly alchemical stone is taken up and worked with, it can turn into something beautiful.

The keloid represents both the earthly substance and its opposite, the spiritual dynamic. Marking the body to invoke the divine cultivates a path to the inner life that reaches across time. The keloids revealed the path I needed to follow in this lifetime and to transition to the next. They were the art that gave me life. They defined me. I would try to incorporate their meaning so my ego could grow into a much larger psyche. That would give the scars their due. They carried a unique message from the ancient psyche. Brought out through ritual, they create a myth.

That myth was now becoming more clear. Discovering the created version of the scar meant to me that I had a chance to purposefully design my life, just as the scarifier deliberately created a beautiful design. By deliberately applying myself to the work, I could transform my life into something more than it had been at the beginning. My central hypothesis evolved from this: that the same archetype underlies both conditions — the spontaneous keloid activity and deliberately carved scars.

The keloid contains the spirit that appears as a physical symptom and the spirit that is carved on the skin. Because the keloid carries such power and numinosity, it is desired by the indigenous soul. The keloid's connection to the divine motivates scarification. The spontaneous scar coming from inside, as if from the Beyond — from the inner realm of the body — equates with the deliberately carved scar that comes from inner inspiration. For the modern day patient with a spontaneous keloid, such alignment with the divine may bring true acceptance of its presence. Disease and design — body symptom and body decoration: two sides of one archetype — they carry the same message.

Historically, scarification is a ritual created to remind man of the gods' power. It creates a link to the transpersonal world that for many modern day people has been lost. For me, the scars were messengers from the transpersonal and my guides to the world beyond this one. The keloids erupt from the primordial psyche, which stands between this world and the next. This autonomous force passes through the body in order to be incarnated. Staying connected to it would prepare me for becoming an ancestor. I could no longer be the child waiting for my mother to come for me. Rather, I must take my place beside her.

Journeying into the land of the ancestors bridged these two worlds, neither of which I had felt was inherently my own. The keloid linked them, as my mother and her death had done. In going to visit "the other world" in Africa I relived my birth on a conscious level. To bring about the necessary effect, I had to experience "the afterlife" in this life. My individuation required that I go all the way into the center of myself and come back out again into a much larger part of myself. But returning to everyday life was uncertain — as uncertain as it had been when I followed my mother into death in my active imagination. Once I was in this "other world," I had a hard time leaving it. A dream I had in Africa just before it was time to come home pointed that out.

*I am being shown a new house to buy, a new living situation. I have been here before. One has to go on a boat to be there. Before it is my turn the boatman raises the post to prevent my entry. I jump in to swim to shore, and then he lowers it. In the new house under construction there are rich red tiles in the kitchen area, and the family is unconditionally accepting, but the intensity is not of my world. I cannot live my own life here. Will I have the stamina, the courage, and good timing to get us out?*

In Africa I found the lost mother, and there I wanted to stay. But I couldn't stay. Nor could I go with the collective boatman "across the river" into death, even though that was my perennial desire. Africa was a taste of the afterworld — similar to my dream of the stone platform in the cavern. Being close to the dying mother is the same as being close to the River Styx. Yet the River Styx refers to transformation.

Just before we left Burkina Faso, our host took us to see his new house under construction. The kitchen had bright red tiles. He and the African people that we met were like a family that was unconditionally accepting. Although I didn't want to leave, I had to bring that experience home. The house in my dream was also an inner house that is still under construction. That meant it represented renewal. But it is not yet complete. I had to continue to build that protective house in a psychological way, stone by stone. In Africa I had been initiated, but I had to have the courage to come back, the courage to live after getting what I had wanted, to emerge from the identity of the poor orphan child and engage in a full life.

The challenge was before me: I had to give back to life what I had been given in the opportunity to go to Africa. An inner shaman was awakened there. Now he spoke with me: "Darkness will challenge the potential new growth, but don't give up. Keep going, and you will continue to find the kin to whom you belong. You can recognize them when you feel the similarities. In the differences reside the challenge of what needs to be integrated in you."

Much had been accomplished in going to the ends of the earth and being able to return. I entered the world "outside time" that I knew when my mother died and where time had stopped for me. To come into the world "of the living" and to continue to see what the Self wanted to see through my eyes was the task before me. Through the keloid, I became more conscious of the Self, and the Self became more conscious of me. It was an offering from the Self, slowly unfolding like a flower and giving the ego permission to do the same. The Self had cultivated the ground for itself to come into life. By offering a connection to the source of my collective beginnings, it reconnected me once again to itself. I had gone full circle.

CHAPTER TEN

# FINDING GOD IN THE SCARS

*The ordinary man is chosen to be the place of God's birth,*
*and in him is incarnated not only (as in Christ) the "light"*
*side of Yahweh: in him God regenerates himself as a totality,*
*in both his light and dark aspects.*[137]

After I came home, an abundance of dreams expressed the transformation taking place inside me. Working with the dreams extended my African adventure. In reformulating the experiences, the psyche was presenting what was "higher" in me, supporting my intention to live out more of my totality.

In one of the first dreams:

> *I am driving between the two main African cities we had*
> *actually visited on our trip. I camp out on a lawn*
> *by the road beside a big house. The woman of the house*
> *comes out and invites me in. She offers to have me join the*
> *family for dinner. The young man who was my guide comes*
> *into the room and sings a song in my honor. It is a song*
> *of love and courage meant as a message and a prayer just for me.*
> *I tell the family if I were to say a blessing before the meal*
> *I would say, "My being here proves the existence of God."*

Being invited into the house in this dream came to me as an antidote to "The Little Match Girl." I no longer had to live that myth. My need to belong was finally satisfied. Africa was the house and the banquet table set before me, what my psyche may have anticipated long ago in the orphan play with my sister.

When I stopped to camp between the two main African cities, psychologically I was camping between the opposites. That meant I was independent and, in that state, less concerned about abandonment. I was just camping, and there was nothing expected; I was on my own, and that was the main thing. When one is independent, one tends to be sought after, rather than when one is hoping for it. The guide, an animus who makes the connection to the Self, sings a song in my honor. He has understood something about eros. He is a loving animus, a male spirit inside who can love for love's sake and not expect anything in return. It is in that state of being that the bridge to an experience of God can be made.

A second dream followed:

> *A priestess, representing the feminine version of God,*
> *asked me to be her marriage partner.*
> *She had previously chosen someone else,*
> *but now she wanted to be with me.*
> *Then she asked me to read my African journal to her.*

This priestess was the highest form of the feminine, and her image was now internalized. It felt as if she had always been on a distant shore waiting for me, but I hadn't been ready for her. Now she thought I was ready. She was seeking me. The priestess was an image of the heavenly mother, and our marriage would signify the resolution of the profound mother complex.

The priestess also represented the spiritual significance of the transformation process that was taking place in me. The Self wanted to strengthen my femininity and my ego so that I could permanently connect to the religious aspect within myself. The religious attitude wanted to be lastingly united with consciousness.

A death attended this significant renewal of my inner life. Six weeks after I returned from Africa, my stepmother died. Although we had been geographically distant since I became an adult, she continued to have an influence over my psyche. Before the funeral, I went into my stepmother's apartment to revisit the family belongings. One item stood out among all the rest. A ceramic ballet dancer, nine inches tall, was hanging on the wall. I didn't remember it being in our childhood house, but of all the family heirlooms that I wanted to keep, this dancer was the one I fell in love with and brought home. To my surprise the little flowers on her dress exactly matched the wallpaper in the room where I put her. But even more striking was her costume; one strap on her gown was made of flowers, exactly like my keloid dream (fig. 57).

With a place of honor in her new home, she was like a spirit coming out of the wall, the spirit in my stepmother's psyche to which she herself had no access. Perhaps it was the autonomous spirit that she had feared and unconsciously sensed was present in the scars. In making the journey to Africa I hoped I had rescued both our spirits from their entanglement in the concrete matter of our lives. The ballet dancer represented the opposites at work in her psyche as well as my own. This helped me view my stepmother from another side. She had accepted the mother role under very difficult circumstances, becoming second wife and second mother. In spite of the complexities of our relationship she had cared about my well-being and was proud of my accomplishments.

As I sat silently before the ballet dancer it came to me that my stepmother, too, may have waited until I was sufficiently launched into life before she left (as my father had done), making up for what my

Fig. 57: *The ceramic ballet dancer.*

own mother couldn't do. The synchronicity of these life-and-death events had a calming effect on me, and it comforted me to know that my father and stepmother had stayed around to see me through.

This little figure also reflected the culmination of the alchemical transformation. The red flowers on the white dress represented the darkness at the beginning of the alchemical opus, whitened or purified through analysis that now became the rich red of feelings and the life-giving principle. By pursuing my passion, I had taken a large step out into the world. The keloid opening into a flower and the barren tree giving birth to fruit carried the same message, anticipating this new development. The passions of my creative nature had broken through.

Two other dreams I had a short while later also brought up the alchemical colors of white and red.

> *I am now occupying the closet that had originally been my mother's.*
> *Next it belonged to my stepmother, and now it is my closet.*
> *It contains red choir robes with white lace tops.*

The choir robes related to music. Now, it was my time to sing. The psychological transformation evolving in me was mirrored in the coming together of the alchemical opposites reflected in the red and white. The combination of the two colors represents the *coniunctio*, the union of opposites and a conscious realization of the Self. The unconscious was preparing to celebrate a mass of its own.

This theme was followed up in the next dream I had.

> *My husband and I are walking down the aisle of a church.*
> *It is the end of the ceremony, and the priest is announcing two offerings.*
> *One is represented by a small man being lifted into the lap of another man.*
> *He has two keloids on his arm, one resting on top of the other;*
> *that is the second offering. I say, "I have scars like yours, and*
> *I am interested in scarification." He invites me to his house to talk.*
> *I bring two offerings, red wine and something white, perhaps it is water.*

In his discussion of the Mass, Jung writes about the mixing of water and wine, the red and white, in the preparation of the chalice. He suggests that the water represents our material nature and, mixed with wine, signifies "divinity is mingled with humanity."[138] The water (i.e., what is human) must be purified and perfected, as I was doing in the analysis of the unconscious, to make the ego worthy of sacrifice.

Mixing wine and water represents the opposites; in alchemy red is the male principle, the energy of the drive, and white is the feminine, the drive control or regulation.[139] The red of blame and guilt had transformed into the passions of my creative nature. When I felt out of balance the other principle brought in the wholeness.

In the dream a small man is resting in the arms of a larger man, and this is echoed by the keloid resting on a larger keloid. This image reflected the condition of the ego that does in fact rest in the arms of the Self. It gave me a feeling of resting in myself instead of needing sustenance from the outside. It meant I had everything inside. The ego and Self are of the same material, and the scar is part of that. The doubling of the image means the work is coming out of the world of the unconscious into the world of consciousness. The keloid had given the eternal a solid form, and my research work, by giving me greater understanding, had reinforced the container in which it could live.

Another dream incorporated the principle that what is lower, dark, and in this case "broken," carries the promise of renewal beyond mere restoration.

> *There is a broken plate, and a voice brings the message:*
> *from the shards of the glass where the plate is broken*
> *comes the beginning of the world.*

For the orphan the plate, which is a symbol of the feminine and of sacrifice,[140] has broken apart, and the work of gathering the shards from this break is the sacrifice one makes to restore and create new life. As one makes this sacrifice, one becomes the sacrifice. In the process of analysis, making conscious the dissonant parts of the psyche, one is reduced to shards, to dust, and then renewed once again. From dust to dust we begin and end.

> Then the Lord God formed a man from the dust of
> the ground and breathed into his nostrils the breath
> of life.[141]

Wherever and however one is wounded, the efforts to heal create one's world anew. There is always "a break in the plate" that makes renewed life possible. The psyche that wounds and is wounded can repair itself, just as in the dark of night (in the world of dreams) consciousness descends into the unconscious and is repaired and renewed.

The wounds of experience make a bridge from the beginning of life to its end. In the early years, when the ego is the unreflecting experiment of the Self, the plate seems whole; in the middle years when one endures the trials and challenges of life, analyzing and sorting them out, one experiences the plate as breaking apart. In the later years, when one discovers and integrates the archetypal roots of one's myth, the plate is made whole and is transformed. From the *materia* of the break in my plate, from the brokenness I experienced at birth, came the renewal of my life. It gave me a purpose. By integrating the effects of the break, I could contribute to something larger. In becoming more conscious, differentiating and integrating more aspects of myself, I was renewed. Beyond that, I could help renew life in the people around me.

As with my previous dream involving the shards of glass sticking to my skin, I once again associated shards with the broken pots housing the eternal light that are mentioned in the Kabbalah. Those shards, according to Jung, represent "the forces of evil and darkness." They "form ten counterpoles to the ten *sefiroth,* which are the ten stages in the revelation of God's creative power." Cleansing "the evil admixture" of the shards took place in what is described as the "breaking of the vessels."[142] It is through work with the shadow elements, both dark and light, that one transforms the inferior side and takes it to a higher level. Out of the dark side of life renewal can take place. This is the message of the dream.

This theme is repeated in the next dream I had, of a new baby with a damaged heart that needs repair; and with this repair, the plate replenishes itself.

> *A new baby is having surgery for a damaged heart that needs repair.*
> *In the next room I am passing a plate of food around to an ever-increasing*
> *number of people gathering to help me take care of the baby in her recovery.*
> *I am worried I don't have enough food for all the people, but*
> *as they take food from the plate it is magically replaced by more food.*

My heart was touched in Africa, more deeply than anything I had known. The keloid research was repairing the initial injury and helping me find a new container from which to live. It healed the broken heart I suffered when my mother died. In its continual return to me the keloid had been trying to repair the damage. The work I was doing on its many layers insured its continuing protection and healing. The food that was being replenished on the plate and the ever-increasing number of people who had come to help were metaphors for this ever-renewing source of support from the autonomous psyche. Knowing that there was a well of nourishment stored within and that my efforts would renew the supply, I could develop courage and come into the outer world with enough food to share with others.

This new baby, born from the unconscious, was a divine child that had to be looked after, repaired, and attended to, because the transformation was still not healed or integrated. It needed intensive care, surgery for the damaged heart. As it gets the care that it needs for its well-being, more people come to help me. The plate of food is magically replenished, and I realize I have found something divine. One who finds the nourishment of the unconscious will never starve again. The following dream used my adventure in Africa to describe exquisitely the marrow of this process.

*The experience of Africa was blue liquid in a ladle.*

Going to Africa was going far into the unconscious and reconnecting to the archetypal level in a creative way. The ladle is a container, and it indicates I can contain my experience of Africa. It is the paradox of the greatest and the smallest. In the ladle, I have the whole of Africa, and within that I can contain the whole origin of the psyche, because all humans come from Africa. In addition, the ladle is used to serve something from the main vessel to other individual containers. The dream was saying that I can convey to others what I have been given.

According to the alchemist Gerhard Dorn, blue liquid is the divine water. It is the quintessence of the process. In an alchemical recipe, "residue from a previous operation . . . . is . . . dissolved and rotated until a pure blue liquid comes to the top."[143] It is called *caelum*. Psychologically, the blue liquid evolved from a process of reconnecting emotions (or affects) with consciousness. *Caelum* "was the celestial substance hidden in man, the secret 'truth,' the 'sum of virtue,' the 'treasure which is not eaten into by moths nor dug out by thieves.' In the world's eyes it is the cheapest thing, but 'to the wise more worthy of love than precious stones and gold, a good that passeth not away, and is taken hence after death.'" Jung interprets it as "the immortal part of man."[144]

*Caelum* also refers to "a certain heavenly substance hidden in the human body"[145] that is lured out by the "art." It is the hidden God within that is extracted, the image of God that, once recognized, establishes one in a spiritual position. That is the art of scarification and the art of the inner work. It was the hidden God-image within the scars and within the unconscious that was redeemed in me.

When I returned home from my trip and continued my active imagination with the keloid, God revealed himself as the center of the keloid and the wedding flower of the *coniunctio*. It was a *hierosgamos*, a sacred marriage, and the keloid was the jewel. The keloids were flowers from God. They provided a place for God to enter. In Africa, on foreign soil and away from familiar surroundings, God was born anew into my conscious life. The flower, the work of my flowering, will remain long after I and the scars on my mortal body bloom, wither and die. I will become God's garden.

Jung understood why this poetry was pouring forth in me.

> The state of imperfect transformation, merely hoped for and waited for, does not seem to be one of torment only, but of positive, if hidden, happiness. It is the state of someone who, in his wanderings among the mazes of his psychic transformation, comes upon a secret happiness which reconciles him to his apparent loneliness. In communing with himself he finds not deadly boredom and melancholy but an inner partner; more than that, a relationship that seems like the happiness of a secret love, or like a hidden springtime, when the green seed sprouts from the barren earth, holding out the promise of future harvests.[146]

God is the house I want to live in, and becoming myself means I become the house for God. The flower garden is then inside me. Miraculously, several years after I returned from Africa, that garden emerged from my body in the form of a new scar that developed on my breast. This was not an ordinary scar. It combined with the keloid star that had formed when our son was born (fig. 58). Now it became the image of an animal, with the star as the tip of its tail (fig. 59). I felt it was a sign from God, an affirmation of my work and a symbol of protection. It reminded me of the earlier dream invitation to be with the cave animal in the core of the earth.

To me, the appearance of the animal on my body was the highest badge of honor I could have received. It echoed what Gerhard Dorn

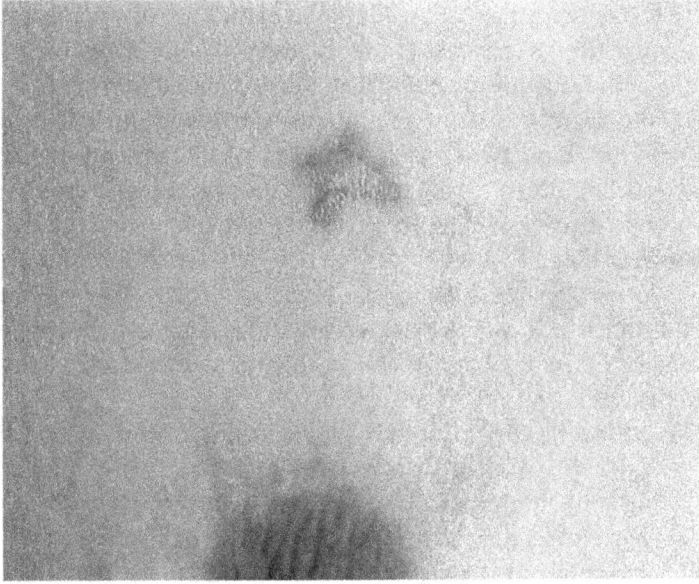

Fig. 58: *The star on my breast.*

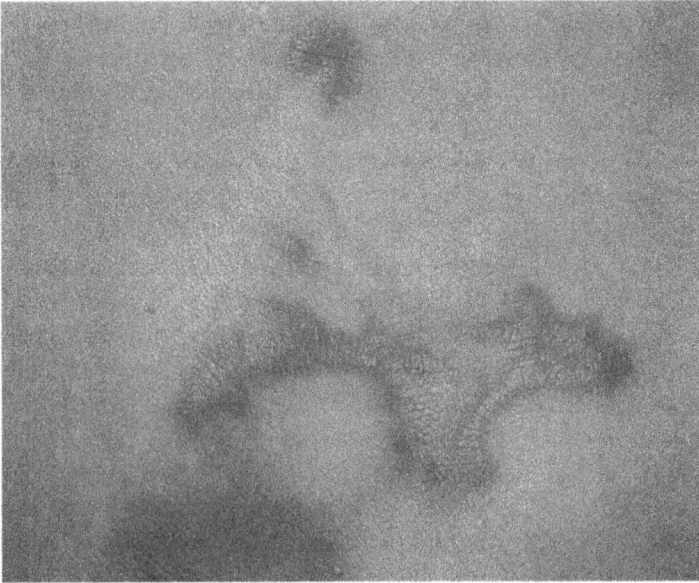

Fig. 59: *The animal on my breast.*

wrote in regard to the motif of election to the faithful of God and the continuing interpenetration of God in his servants.

> For it sometimes comes about, after many years, many labours, much study . . . that some are chosen, when much knocking, ['knock and it shall be opened unto you (Matthew 7:7)'] many prayers, and diligent inquiry have gone before.[147]

Like the indigenous people I met, I experienced the scars as "marks of God," and signs of my connection to all creation. These totems were placed on the body as badges of the god or the community to which one belonged. Animal scars are carved when the young men come of age and are initiated into warrior groups, each with a different pattern of scars (figs. 60–62). The initiated groups gather together to participate in village activities and for the hunt. My star and the protective spirit force were alive inside me. My animal was an authentication of my life's work. Like a totem animal that represents belonging to a group or to a deity, this animal signified that I belonged to God. Spirit had descended into matter and arose from matter.

To the ancient Jews, marks on the body represented a covenant with God. "The ultimate Semitic root is the same for 'mark' and 'covenant' (cf. the Arabic *sharat*, 'a mark,' and *shart*, 'a covenant')."[148] In the Old Testament (Ezekial 9:1–6), God dictates that a protecting mark be placed on the foreheads of those who "groan and lament over the abominations practised" in Jerusalem, while all the others are to be killed "without pity."[149] Sacrifice and marking as protection come together in the famous Passover in Egypt, when God tells Moses to take the blood of a goat or sheep "and smear it on the two doorposts and on the lintel of every house" (Exodus 12:7–8) and says that "the blood will be a sign on the houses in which you are: when I see the blood I will pass over you . . . when I strike the land of Egypt" (Exodus 12:13).[150]

Cain was also protected with God's mark. "Cain said to the Lord, 'My punishment is heavier than I can bear; thou has driven me today from the ground, and I must hide myself from thy presence. I shall be a vagrant and a wanderer on earth, and anyone who meets me can kill me.' The Lord answered him, 'No: if anyone kills Cain, Cain shall be avenged sevenfold.' So the Lord put a mark on Cain, in order that anyone meeting him should not kill him" (Genesis 4:13–16).[151]

Fig. 60: *Carving an animal design. Reprinted from* The Last of the Nuba *by Leni Riefenstahl: New York, St. Martin's Press, 1995, © Leni Riefenstahl), by permission of Leni Riefenstahl - Produktion.*

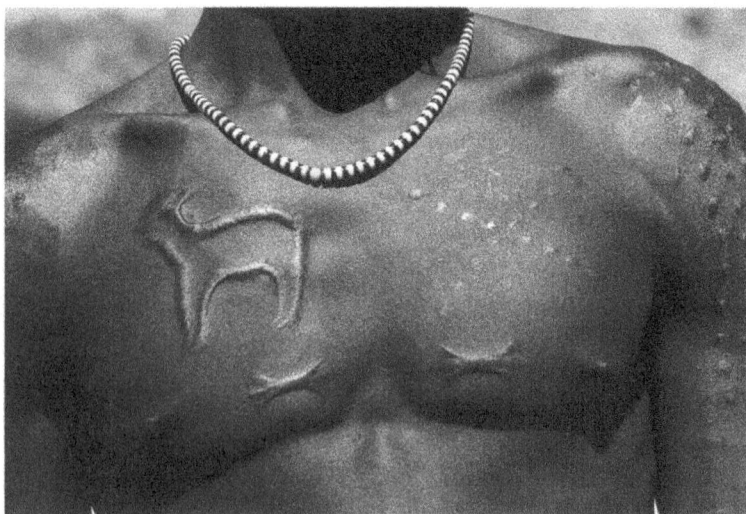

Fig. 61: *An animal scar. Reprinted from* The Last of the Nuba *by Leni Riefenstahl: New York, St. Martin's Press, 1995, © Leni Riefenstahl, by permission of Leni Riefenstahl - Produktion.*

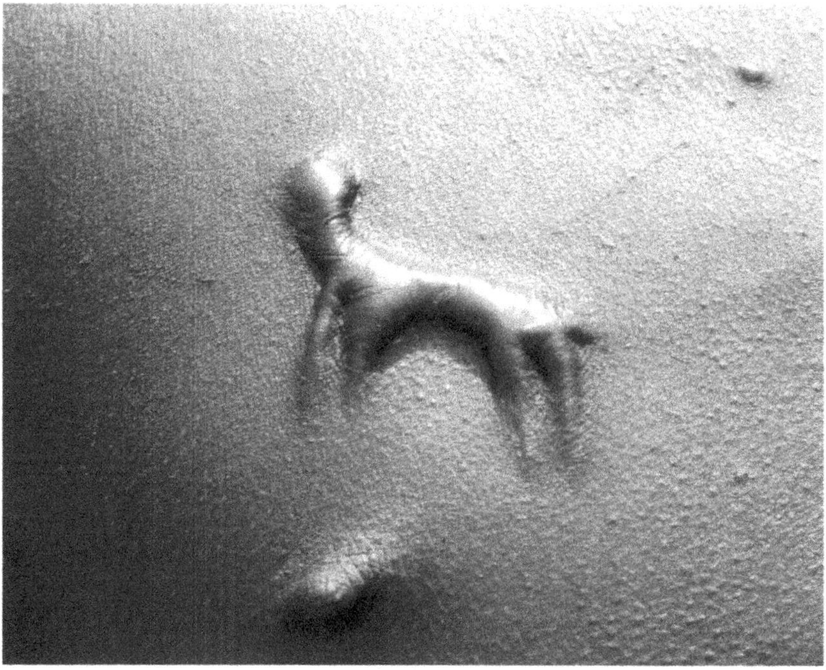

Fig. 62: *Keloid in the form of an animal. Reprinted from* The Last of the Nuba *by Leni Riefenstahl: New York, St. Martin's Press, 1995. © Leni Riefenstahl, by permission of Leni Riefenstahl - Produktion.*

"Lineally descended from these, too, is perhaps the badge referred to in Job 31:35 ('Lo, here is my mark, let the Almighty answer me.'). The word used here for 'mark' comes from the root meaning 'to wound,' and it is the same as that used in Ezekiel 9:4–6, the reference being to those who are true to God, and therefore belong to Him."[152]

In *The Creation of Consciousness*, Edward Edinger says that Yahweh, who wants to incarnate in man, "manifests himself on man's skin" and mentions Job "who risked his skin to contend with God."[153] Discussing the flaying of the skin in association with a dream image of an oracle appearing on a flayed skin, he goes on to write, "This image is relevant to everyone who submits himself to the process of individuation. He will be offering up his 'skin' to be a kind of vellum manuscript on which Yahweh writes his revelation."[154]

The symbol of the keloid and its life in me could not be stated more clearly than in this final dream.

*I peeled the scars off my arm. They looked like a cluster of grapes.*

In the earlier dream my friend, whose relationship to me brought about a transformation, had eaten the scars as grapes. Now it was time to bring the transformation into being myself, and that meant my whole life had to be lived in honor of my new consciousness of the sacred element in me that led me where I needed to go. The keloids were the *prima materia,* and the grapes were the *lapis,* the completion of the process. The keloids becoming grapes symbolized the transformation of something ordinary, and even despised, into something divine. The divinity of the grape and its organic nature were a part of me. I belonged to all of creation. I belonged to all of time. I had missed nothing.

# AFTERWORD

*. . . the raising of the jewel, the thing that always comes from below . . . . the divine process which goes on within us, [parallels] our ordinary psychological processes.*[155]

I have come to appreciate that one reason darkness is given to us is to challenge us to be continually reborn out of the darkness, to find ourselves anew. This relates to the profound psychological principle that new life begins with what is "lowest." Jung put it this way.

> [The god] appears at first in hostile form, as an assailant with whom the hero has to wrestle. This is in keeping with the violence of all unconscious dynamism . . . . the fight against the paralyzing grip of the unconscious calls forth man's creative powers. That is the source of all creativity, but it needs heroic courage to do battle with these forces and to wrest from them the treasure hard to attain."[156]

In my case, the death of my mother, the coming of my stepmother, and the appearance of the scars were part of this creative process and constitute examples of "what is lowest." The "assailants" with whom I had to wrestle held what was missing in me, namely, the unborn parts that were not initiated by my mother. Then the challenge became: how could I express these newly born parts of myself and bring them into life?

From a very young age, this work seemed imperative. Standing on the edge of the swimming pool at day camp, each five-year-old camper had to jump into the swimming pool in order to earn a frog badge. I was too afraid to jump in. Later that day, when I was walking up the street with my stepmother, I told her what had happened that morning at the pool, and I started to cry. I wanted that frog badge more than anything. I wanted to be like all the other kids. My stepmother responded, "I'll buy you a frog badge." "No!" I said. I knew, even then, that it didn't feel right. I didn't want it if I hadn't earned it.

That spirit inside me soon formed itself into the keloid scar and was later channeled into the passionate desire to discover its meaning. The impetus to do the work defied the predictions that I wouldn't make it in the world — that I should stay back, in the "paralyzing grip of the unconscious," as Jung says. The work required me to defy the inner demons. Even though *I* felt inferior, I knew that my *unconscious* was not inferior; *it* had creative energies. That was what I had to hold onto. Bringing these creative energies into action gave my life purpose and meaning. Rather than seeing myself as inferior by identifying with what was missing in me, or what I missed on the outside, I began to see that the Self needed to repair itself *through* me and needed *me* to carry a connection to *it*. The creative instinct born from the unconscious had evoked in me a conscious willingness to carry my own inner authority. I didn't need to ask permission from an outer authority to proceed. Then I was able to grow into the next, more expansive level of my life. My compelling interest overrode the complexes, and I was able to undertake this task. Each time I was able to move forward, I transformed another piece of darkness; this in turn allowed me greater freedom to carry out the work. The pleasure that filled me when I did anything related to this material demonstrated that the positive side of myself was finally able to live.

The keloid scars were an expression of my fate as a motherless child. I later understood that carrying the keloid scars was a privilege. They came to honor the life-and-death equation that leaves its permanent mark. My body provided me with a way to transform the chaos at the beginning. Through my fascination with the meaning of the early disfiguring scar, I was led to a more "configured" life, mirroring the intentionally carved scar.

Finding the photographs of the Mesopotamian figurine was the turning point, a hint of something far larger that could redeem my suffering and reveal the mystery behind the scars. (As my analyst once said, "One can bear almost anything if one can see it in its larger context.") Up until that time, I was unanchored, subject to the chaos one experiences when possessed by many forces. I felt I hadn't been fully initiated into the world and didn't entirely belong here. Yet the unconscious was spurring me on to further realize myself.

It was only after understanding their metaphysical, spiritual, and symbolic meanings that the scars became flowers for me. They continued to guide *me*, through my continuing interest in *them* — to study, to travel, and most importantly, to develop and incorporate more and more of myself into what I am today. As the years unfolded, my research turned to writing and to speaking. My strengths came to the forefront, and a solid sense of myself emerged. People with similar issues, or those who felt I could be sympathetic to their unique issues, came to talk with me. I found a sense of purpose. A quiet place inside myself began to manifest. I had found a way to help others discover their own jewels hidden in symptoms and complexes and to realize that the goal of this work on illness is transformation.

What begins in the depths, in the darkness, in the unconscious, in uncharted territory seems to await our attentive ear. It beckons to be embellished with the spirit of our imagination. We shape our relationship to it in an individual way. The Self depends on us to do this, and we are necessary to *it*. Our ongoing dialogue with the symptom and its symbolic expression is part of this process and brings it to life. From these insights evolves further clarity relevant to both psyche and body: what comes from the unconscious and the body is often undervalued and despised. Because it is viewed as worthless, it is easily rejected.

The creative work on one's own symptoms transforms this state of mind. To integrate the deeper layers of the psyche, the intensity of the exploration into the body symptom has to equal the intensity of the forces that created the symptom in the first place. In other words, the intensity that gave rise to the symptom has to be met by an equal intensity of energy focused upon it. This work emerges in response to our suffering, the suffering that serves as an irritant like that which brings the pearl its beauty. It is not what one is given that matters, but one's reaction, attention, and responsibility to what is given. When we find the treasure in such conditions and its mystery is revealed, our energy is renewed, and we can live out the new patterns that have been discovered. The jewel may be lost once again, but it *is* there and awaits rediscovery.

Through the journey the unconscious lends a hand, providing a compensatory symbol to reestablish a proper balance. The unconscious sends inspiration for the troubled soul — a clarifying image, a supportive dream. These are experiences of grace, of a heavenly containment. They lift our spirits because they come from beyond the ego, from something far greater that opens us to a deeper level of the psyche. The unconscious guides us to what needs to be integrated and puts us in touch with the eternal. From this we can draw strength, for this process involves an encounter with the Self, the companion who sustains us in a relationship to the inner world that transcends our limited existence.

When the inner voice speaks, we have encountered something divine. We know we are in the service of something immense. When that message is taken up and worked with, it contributes to our unique myth, the ground of our very being. This myth is in our safe-keeping. It is a life-long assignment for each of us to bring it into consciousness. This is the continuing work, the task that lets the creative force live on. It is born as an inspiration, coming from the realm of the unconscious and the Mother, the womb of the psyche. To make the sacred visible and conscious is to discover and retrieve the jewel in the wound.

# NOTES

CW refers to *The Collected Works of C.G. Jung*, trans R.F.C. Hull, ed. H. Read, M. Fordham, G. Adler, Wm. McGuire, Bollingen Series XX (Princeton: Princeton University Press, 1953–1979).

PREFACE, pages 13-15

[1] The collective unconscious is the stratum of the unconscious which, being held in common by all humanity, serves as a wellspring of universal symbols. Its center, the Self, unifies the psyche and functions as an organizing principle of psychological life.

[2] A projection is the "process whereby an unconscious quality or content of one's own is perceived and reacted to in an outer object." Edward F. Edinger, *Melville's Moby-Dick: A Jungian Commentary* (New York: New Directions, 1978), p. 149.

[3] Stanislas Klossowski de Rola. *Alchemy: The Secret Art* (London: Thames and Hudson, 1973), fig. 61.

[4] C.G. Jung and C. Kerényi, *Essays on a Science of Mythology* (New York: Harper & Row, 1963), p. 103.

INTRODUCTION, pages 18-22

[5] An archetype is the innate form underlying universal and recurring images, patterns of behavior and mythological motifs.

[6] The archetypal layer is the deepest layer of the collective unconscious. It generates the universal symbols in dreams, myths, fairytales, religion, etc.

[7] Jung, *Alchemical Studies*, CW 13, par. 242.

[8] C.G. Jung, *Dream Analysis: Notes of the Seminar Given in 1928–1930* (Princeton NJ: Princeton University Press, 1984), p. 20.

[9] Jolande Jacobi (ed.), *Paracelsus: Selected Writings* (Princeton, NJ: Princeton University Press, 1951), pp. 76, 78.

[10] The method of active imagination involves actively participating in a dialogue with images that come up from the unconscious. A direct

response from the ego, through some form of expression, such as clay, painting, or writing establishes a living relationship with the inner world. An excellent discussion of active imagination can be found in Barbara Hannah, *Encounters with the Soul: Active Imagination as Developed by C.G. Jung* (Santa Monica: Sigo Press, 1981).

## CHAPTER 1, pages 23-36

[11] C.G. Jung, *Memories, Dreams, Reflections* (New York: Random House, 1963), p. 325.

[12] Kira Melissarato, *Wee Fishie Wun*, illustrated by John V. Schwarzman (New York: Cupples & Leon Company, 1945).

[13] A complex is an emotionally charged, unconscious entity composed of a number of associated ideas grouped around a central core, which is an archetypal image. One recognizes that a complex has been activated when emotion upsets psychic balance and disturbs the customary function of the ego.

[14] An earlier version of this material first appeared in my article, "The Orphan Archetype," *Psychological Perspectives*, 14, no. 1 (Fall 1983): 181–194, reprinted in Jeremiah Abrams (ed.), *Reclaiming the Inner Child* (Los Angeles: Jeremy P. Tarcher, Inc., 1990), pp. 87-97.

[15] Lynd Ward, *Gods' Man* (New York: Jonathan Cape and Harrison Smith, 1929).

## CHAPTER 2, pages 37-52

[16] Marie-Louise von Franz, ed. *Aurora Consurgens* (London: Routledge & Kegan Paul, 1966), p. 262.

[17] Jung, *Psychology and Alchemy*, CW 12, par. 101.

[18] Jung, *Mysterium Coniunctionis*, CW 14, pars. 13, 14.

[19] C.G. Jung, *Memories, Dreams, Reflections*, p. 226.

[20] *Ibid.*, p. 227.

[21] *Ibid.*

[22] Erich Neumann, *The Child* (New York: G.P. Putnam's Sons, 1973), p. 86.

23 Jung, *Symbols of Transformation*, CW 5, par. 553.

24 Hans Christian Andersen, *The Little Match Girl* (New York: G.P. Putnam's Sons, 1987).

25 Erich Neumann, *The Child* , p. 72.


CHAPTER 3, pages 53-65

26 Jung, *Alchemical Studies*, CW 13, pars. 396, 397.

27 Iona and Peter Opie, *The Classic Fairy Tales* (New York: Oxford University Press, 1974), pp. 241–244.

28 Shakespeare, *As You Like It*, act 2, scene 1, lines 12–17, eds. Herschel Baker et al., *The Riverside Shakespeare* (New York: Houghton Mifflin, 1997), p. 410.

29 C.G. Jung. *The Visions Seminars* (Zurich: Spring Publications, 1976), vol. 1, pp. 202–204.

30 William Morris, ed. *The American Heritage Dictionary of the English Language* (New York: American Heritage Publishing Co., 1969), p. 241.

31 The Egyptian god, Horus, who, as the child, "arises from the expanding lotus growing on the breast of the primeval deep" (typifying the sun reborn each morning) [Ad de Vries, *Dictionary of Symbols and Imagery* (Amsterdam: North-Holland Publishing Co., 1974), p. 305] is "symbolic of the power which leads the soul from darkness, death and ignorance to the mansions of the blessed." This represents the transformation of nature to a higher spiritual principle. [Gertrude Jobes, *Dictionary of Mythology Folklore and Symbols* (New York: The Scarecrow Press, Inc., 1962), part 1, p. 792.]

32 Nathaniel Hawthorne, "The Birth-mark," *Tales and Sketches* (New York: Library Classics of the United States Inc., 1982), pp. 764–780, at 777.

33 The anima is the unconscious feminine aspect in a man's psyche, and the animus is the unconscious masculine side of the woman.

34 Joseph Campbell, *The Mythic Image* (Princeton: Princeton University Press, 1974), p. 249.

CHAPTER 4, pages 66-79

[35] Jung, *Symbols of Transformation*, CW 5, par. 644.

[36] Jung, *The Archetypes and the Collective Unconscious*, CW 9-1, par. 576. Jung noted that "[t]he lotus seat of the Horus-child, of the Indian divinities, and of the Buddha must be understood in this sense....In Christian metaphor, Mary is the flower in which God lies hidden...." CW 9-1, pars. 576-577.

[37] Robert Jay Lifton, *Death in Life: Survivors of Hiroshima* (New York: Basic Books, Inc., 1967), pp. 177–178.

[38] *Ibid.*, p. 18l.

[39] Jung, *The Symbolic Life*, CW 18, pars. 1094–1095.

[40] Hans Andersen's fairy tale "The Snow Queen" has as its central theme the shards of glass resulting from the break in the wicked hobgoblin's mirror. If a splinter entered one's eye, he saw everything askew. If it entered the heart, it turned the person cold. The shedding of tears melts the ice. Andrew Lang (ed.), *The Pink Fairy Book* (New York: Dover Publications, Inc., 1967), pp. 76–101.

[41] Edward Edinger, *The Eternal Drama* (Boston: Shambhala Publications, 1994), p. 141.

[42] Robert Graves, *The Greek Myths* (Middlesex, England: Penguin Books, Inc., 1973), vol. 2, pp. 73–79.

[43] *Ibid.*, p. 76.

[44] *Ibid.*, p. 58.

[45] *Ibid.*, p. 60.


CHAPTER 5, pages 80-95

[46] Donald Sandner, *Proceedings of the 1985 California Spring Conference of Jungian Analysts and Control Candidates* (San Francisco: C.G. Jung Institute of San Francisco, 1985), pp. 207–210, at 209. (Response to my paper, "Psychic Wounds and Body Scars: An Exploration into the Psychology of Keloid Formation," pp. 189–205.)

[47] Eva Strommenger and Max Hirmer, *The Art of Mesopotamia* (London: Thames and Hudson, 1964), fig 12.

[48] Jung, *Aion*, CW 9-2, pars. 172-174.

[49] Active imagination, a dialogue between the ego and the unconscious, can be used in working with body symptoms. The voice from the 'inner body' is often difficult to access, for the psyche is deeply veiled in matter. Yet it seems to respond to one's sincere interest. One is dependent on the cooperation of the unconscious to make the journey into the core of the symptom to find whatever light may be hidden within. The ego becomes a participant in activating healing and attempts to meet the unknown forces half way.

[50] The alchemists discussed the "Crucified Mercurial Serpent" and illustrated it nailed on a pole like the image of Christ on the cross. Among other things, it means that the incarnation of God in a human person, i.e. the individuation process (or, the snake that descended into me), "fixes" one to his own cross, to the responsibility of his own life. See Edward F. Edinger, *Anatomy of the Psyche* ( La Salle, IL: Open Court, 1985), pp. 104-107; and C.G. Jung, "The Philosophical Tree" in *Alchemical Studies*, CW 13, pars. 304–482. The snake leaving the flask and entering the human body can also be seen as a collective image that may signify that human beings endure God's suffering, as Christ endured God's suffering, for the sake of transformation. The snake's moving into the body and incubating there, as a disease, relates to the god's incarnation for the sake of rebirth and renewal.

[51] C.G. Jung, *Dream Analysis*, p. 248.

[52] Mircea Eliade, *Rites and Symbols of Initiation* (New York: Harper & Row, 1958), p. 89.

[53] The snake enters the picture when the libidinal urge of the Self needs to be heard and incarnated. Edward F. Edinger [*Ego and Archetype* (Baltimore: Penguin Books Inc., 1973), pp. 80–81] says about this: "The serpent played the same role [for Job as] for Adam and Eve in the Garden of Eden....Such an image heralds an individuation crisis, a major step in psychological development which requires that old conditions be destroyed to make room for the new. Destructive or liberating effects may predominate, usually there is a mixture of both."

[54] C.G. Jung, *Nietzsche's Zarathustra: Notes of the Seminar Given in 1934–1939*, ed. James L. Jarrett (Princeton: Princeton University Press, 1988), vol. 2, pp. 1061–1062.

[55] C.G. Jung, *Memories, Dreams, Reflections*, p. 227.

[56] Jung, *Alchemical Studies*, CW 13, par. 101(n).

[57] Jung, *Aion*, CW 9–2, par. 214.

[58] Edward F. Edinger, *Anatomy of the Psyche*, p. 154.


CHAPTER 6, pages 96-113

[59] Jung, *The Spirit In Man, Art, And Literature*, CW 15, par. 4.

[60] Jung, *Mysterium Coniunctionis*, CW 14, par 21.

[61] Personal communication with Edward Edinger.

[62] In *Ego and Archetype*, p. 132, Edward Edinger writes about a hole that is left in the psyche when there is no personal parent to mediate between the ego and the image of the archetypal [mother]. Through that hole can emerge "powerful archetypal contents of the collective unconscious."

[63] Jung, *Alchemical Studies*, CW 13, par. 186.

[64] *Ibid.*

[65] Jung, *The Archetypes and the Collective Unconscious*, CW 9–1, par. 286.

[66] Jung, *Mysterium Coniunctionis*, CW 14, par. 295.

[67] George F. Elder discusses this myth in his book, *The Body*. The nursemaid is the disguised ogre, Putana, and Krishna's father is King Kamsa. See *The Body: An Encyclopedia of Archetypal Symbolism* (Boston: Shambhala, 1996), vol. 2, pp. 19–20.

[68] Jung, *The Development of Personality*, CW 17, par. 321.


CHAPTER 7, pages 114-138

[69] Jung, *Psychology and Religion: West and East*, CW 11, par. 410.

[70] Tina S. Alster, "Laser Treatment of Hypertrophic Scars, Keloids, and Striae," *Dermatologic Clinics* 15 (1997): 419–429; David A. Sherris, Wayne F. Larrabee, Jr, and Craig S. Murakami, "Management of Scar Contractures, Hypertrophic Scars and Keloids," *Otolaryngologic Clinics of North America* 28 (1995): 1057–1068; Brian Berman and Harlan C. Bieley, "Adjunct Therapies to Surgical Management of Keloids," *Dermatologic Surgery* 22 (1996): 126–130; and Tina S. Alster and Tina B. West, "Treatment of Scars: A Review, "*Annals of Plastic Surgery* 39

(1997):418–432. More recent articles include Harold C. Slavkin, "The Body's Skin Frontier and the Challenges of Wound Healing: Keloids," *Journal of the American Dental Association* 131 (2000): 362–365; Robert S. English and Philip D. Shenefelt, "Keloids and Hypertrophic Scars," *Dermatologic Surgery* 25 (1999): 631–638; and F.B. Niessen, P.H. Spauwen, J. Schalkwijk, and M. Kon, "On the Nature of Hypertrophic Scars and Keloids: a Review," *Plastic and Reconstructive Surgery* 104(5) (1999):1435–1458.

[71] David Bloom, "Heredity of Keloids: Review of the Literature and Report of a Family with Multiple Keloids in Five Generations," *New York State Journal of Medicine* 56 (1956): 511–519.

[72] An earlier version of this material on keloids appears in my article, "Psychic Wounds and Body Scars: An Exploration into the Psychology of Keloid Formation," which was published in *Spring* (1986): 141–154.

[73] Walter B. Shelley, *Consultations in Dermatology with Walter B. Shelley* (Philadelphia: W. B. Saunders Company, 1972), vol. 1, p. 282, quoting "Alibert, the great French dermatologist who described and named this common tumor in 1806–1817."

[74] Albert R. McFarland, quoted in "Discussion" in David Bloom, "Heredity of Keloids" at 519.

[75] J.-L. Grignon, G. Schneck, and D. Gross, "La Mauvaise Cicatrice Cutanée: Punition ou destin?" *Revue De Stomatologie* 68 (1967): 622–635.

[76] Walter B. Shelley, *Consultations*, p. 284.

[77] P. Omo-Dare, "Yoruban Contributions to the Literature on Keloids," *Journal of the National Medical Association* 65 (1973): 367–372, 406, at 372.

[78] See Helen M. Luke, *Kaleidoscope: "The Way of Woman" and Other Essays* (New York: Parabola Books, 1992), pp. 207–209.

[79] Jung, *Mysterium Coniunctionis*, CW 14, par. 476.

[80] Job 30:17 The Jerusalem Bible.

[81] Jung, *Psychology and Religion: West and East*, CW 11, par. 525.

[82] C.G. Jung, *Dream Analysis*, p. 379.

[83] See, generally, Marija Gimbutas, *The Goddesses and Gods of Old Europe* (London: Thames and Hudson, 1982).

[84] Adrienne Mayor, "People Illustrated," *Archaeology* (March/April,

1999): 54–57, at 57.

[85] Michel Thévoz, *The Painted Body* (Geneva: Editions d'Art Albert Skira S.A., 1984), p. 62.

[86] See, generally, Marija Gimbutas, *The Language of the Goddess* (San Francisco: Harper & Row, 1989).

[87] See, generally, Michael Kan, Clement Meighan, H.B. Nicholson, *Sculpture of Ancient West Mexico: Nayarit, Jalisco, Colima* (Los Angeles: Los Angeles County Museum of Art and University of New Mexico, 1989).

[88] Ekpo Eyo and Frank Willett, *Treasures of Ancient Nigeria* (New York: Alfred A. Knopf, 1982), figs. 42, 43, 47, 48, pp. 94–95, 100–101.

[89] Cornelius O. Adepegba, "A Survey of Nigerian Body Markings And Their Relationship To Other Nigerian Arts" (Ph.D. dissertation, Indiana University, 1976), pp. 17–18, quoting Samuel Johnson, *The History of the Yorubas* (Westport, Conn.: Negro Universities Press, 1970 [reprint of 1921 edition]), p. 150.

[90] *Ibid.*, p. 18, quoting Gerald Neher, "Creative Expression in Arts and Crafts," in Chalmer Faw, ed., *Lardin Gabas: A Land, A People, and A Church* (Elgin, Ill.: The Brethren Press, 1973), p. 69.

[91] See, generally, Arnold Rubin (ed.), *Marks of Civilization* (Los Angeles: Museum of Cultural History, 1988).

[92] Leni Riefenstahl, *The People of Kau* (New York: Harper and Row, 1976), pp. 221–222.

[93] *Ibid.*

[94] R. Brough Smyth, *The Aborigines of Victoria: With Notes Relating to the Habits of the Natives of Other Parts of Australia and Tasmania* (London: Trubner and Co., 1878), pp. 66–68.

[95] Victoria Ebin, *The Body Decorated* (London: Thames and Hudson, 1979), fig. 56.

[96] Bruce Lincoln, *Emerging from the Chrysalis: Studies in Rituals of Women's Initiation* (Cambridge, MA: Harvard University Press, 1981), pp. 46–49.

[97] Mary Nooter Roberts and Allen F. Roberts, *Luba Art and the Making of History* (New York: The Museum for African Art, 1996), p. 111.

[98] Personal communication with Douchan Gersi.

[99] Editors of Time-Life Books, *The Spirit World* (Alexandria, Va.: Time-Life Books, 1992), p. 155.

[100] Marla C. Burns, "Ga'anda Scarification: A Model for Art and Identity," in Arnold Rubin (ed.), *Marks of Civilization*, (Los Angeles: Museum of Cultural History, 1988), p. 65

[101] *Ibid.*, p. 72.

[102] Carol Beckwith and Angela Fisher, *African Ceremonies* (New York: Harry N. Abrams, Inc., 1999), vol. 1, p. 254.

[103] *Ibid.*, vol. 2, p. 83.

[104] Constance Jenkinson, "Tatuing," in James Hastings, ed., *Encyclopedia of Religion and Ethics* (Edinburgh: T. and T. Clark, 1921), vol. 12, pp. 208–214, at 211–212.

[105] *Ibid.*, p. 212.

[106] Stanley D. Porteus, *The Psychology of a Primitive People: A Study of the Australian Aborigine* (London: Edward Arnold and Co., 1931), p.121.

[107] Theodor Waitz and Georg Gerland, "The Peoples of the South Seas, Part III," *Anthropologie der Naturvölker* 6 (1872): 37.

[108] Personal communication with Douchan Gersi.

[109] Peter Gathercole, "Contexts of Maori Moko," in Arnold Rubin (ed.), *Marks of Civilization*, pp. 171–177.

[110] Joy Gritton, "Labrets and Tattooing in Native Alaska," in Arnold Rubin (ed.), *Marks of Civilization*, pp. 181–190, at pp. 188–189.

[111] *Ibid.*, p. 188.

[112] Constance Jenkinson, "Tatuing," at p. 213.

[113] Elizabeth Austin, "Marks of Mystery," *Psychology Today* (July/August 1999): 46–49, 78–79, 82, at 49, quoting Kevin McAleer, *Dueling: The Cult of Honor in Fin-de-Siècle Germany* (Princeton: Princeton University Press, 1997).

[114] Adrienne Mayor, "People Illustrated," p. 54.

[115] Donald McCallum, "Historical and Cultural Dimensions of the Tattoo in Japan," in Arnold Rubin (ed.), *Marks of Civilization*, pp. 109–134.

[116] *Ibid.*

[117] Lewis Spence, "Circumcision (American)," in James Hastings, ed., *Encyclopedia of Religion and Ethics*, vol. 3, p. 670.

[118] George A. Barton, "Circumcision (Semitic)," in James Hastings, ed.,

*Encyclopedia of Religion and Ethics*, vol. 3, pp. 679–680, at 680.

[119] H. Cowan, "Stigmata," in James Hastings, ed., *Encyclopedia of Religion and Ethics*, vol. 11, pp. 857–860, at 857.

[120] *Ibid.*

[121] Allen F. Roberts, "Tabwa Tegumentary Inscription," in Arnold Rubin (ed.), *Marks of Civilization*, pp. 41–56.

[122] *Ibid.*, p. 41, 43.

[123] Edward F. Edinger, *Anatomy of the Psyche*, p. 9.

[124] J.E. Cirlot, *A Dictionary of Symbols* (New York: Philosophical Library, 1962), p. 312.

[125] John Leo, "The 'modern primitives,'" *U.S. News and World Report*, 31 July 1995, 16 (quoting unidentified source).

[126] *Ibid.*

[127] George R. Elder, *The Body*, p. 61.

[128] Robert Brian, *The Decorated Body* (New York: Harper & Row, 1979), p. 160.

[129] W.H.D. Rouse (trans.), Eric H. Warmington and Philip G. Rouse (eds.), *Great Dialogues of Plato* (New York: The New American Library, Inc., 1956), pp. 415–417.


CHAPTER 8, pages 139-160

[130] Jung, *Psychology and Religion: West and East*, CW 11, par. 397.

[131] *Jung, Mysterium Coniunctionis*, CW 14, par. 279.

[132] Jung, *Psychology and Religion: West and East*, CW 11, par. 398.

[133] C.G. Jung, *Memories, Dreams, Reflections*, p. 253.

[134] Carol Beckwith and Angela Fisher, *African Ceremonies* (New York: Harry N. Abrams, Inc., 1999), vol. 2, pp. 13, 99: "In many African cultures, the use of masks and masquerades dramatize the ways in which the seasons and the natural order are honored. During these vibrant rituals, spirits representing the forces of nature enter the masks to bring them to life. Crafted largely from wood, leafy branches and raffia fiber, these nature masks were originally used in early agri-

cultural purification rituals. They evolved from the belief that nature is essentially benevolent and that farming is an offense against this goodness. Despite their efforts to atone for this transgression, early agriculturists believed that on their own they could not be saved from punishment, so they created the first society of masks, whose task was to purify the earth and all those who had defiled it. With time, the masks assumed a broader role and introduced the power of the spirit world into other aspects of life, including initiations, funerals, and other community rituals. . .[T]he masks act as emissaries of man, while still remaining entities of the bush. An artful synthesis of the two worlds, they are regarded as the perfect conciliators in all spiritual matters."

CHAPTER 9, pages 161-177

[135] From the interview with Malidoma Somé.

[136] Eve De Negri, "Tribal marks-decorative scars and painted patterns," *Nigeria Magazine* 81 (1964): 107–116.

CHAPTER 10, pages 178-190

[137] Marie-Louise von Franz, *Aurora Consurgens*, p. 233.

[138] Jung, *Psychology and Religion: West and East*, CW 11, par. 312.

[139] Marie-Louise von Franz, *Aurora Consurgens*, p. 305.

[140] Ad de Vries, *Dictionary of Symbols and Imagery* (Amsterdam: North-Holland Publishing Company, 1974), p. 369.

[141] Gen. 2:7 *The New English Bible* [NEB].

[142] Jung, *Psychology and Religion: West and East*, CW 11, par. 595, n.8, quoting Gershom G. Scholem, *Major Trends in Jewish Mysticism* (New York: Schocken Books, 1965), p. 267.

[143] Edward F. Edinger, *The Mysterium Lectures: A Journey through C.G. Jung's Mysterium Coniunctionis*, ed. Joan Dexter Blackmer (Toronto: Inner City Books, 1995), p. 287.

[144] Jung, *Mysterium Coniunctionis*, CW 14, par. 693 and n.104, quoting Dorn, "Phil. medit.," pp. 457f.

[145] *Ibid.*, par. 681.

[146] *Ibid.*, par. 623.

[147] *Ibid.*, par. 529, quoting Gerhard Dorn, "Phys. Trismegisti," *Theatr. chem.*, I, p. 413.

[148] W.O.E. Oesterley, "Badges," in James Hastings, ed., *Encyclopedia of Religion and Ethics,* vol. 2, pp. 325–328, at 326–327.

[149] Ezek. 9:1–6 NEB.

[150] Exod. 12:7–8,13 NEB.

[151] Gen. 4:13–16 NEB.

[152] W.O.E. Oesterley, "Badges," at p. 327.

[153] Edward F. Edinger, *The Creation of Consciousness* (Toronto: Inner City Books, 1984), p. 88.

[154] *Ibid.*


AFTERWORD, pages 191-194

[155] C.G. Jung. *The Visions Seminars*, vol. 2, p. 292.

[156] Jung, *Symbols of Transformation,* CW 5, pars. 523–524.

# SELECTED BIBLIOGRAPHY

## BOOKS

Adepegba, Cornelius O. 1976. "A Survey of Nigerian Body Markings and Their Relationship to Other Nigerian Arts" (unpublished Ph.D. dissertation, Dept. of Fine Arts, Indiana University).

Andersen, Hans Christian, ill. Rachel Isadora. 1987. *The Little Match Girl*. New York: G.P. Putnam's Sons.

Beckwith, Carol and Fisher, Angela. 1999. *African Ceremonies*. New York: Harry N. Abrams, Inc., 2 vols.

Brian, Robert. 1979. *The Decorated Body*. New York: Harper & Row.

Campbell, Joseph. 1974. *The Mythic Image*. Princeton: Princeton University Press.

Cirlot, J.E. 1962. *A Dictionary of Symbols*. New York: Philosophical Library.

de Rola, Stanislas Klossowski. 1973. *Alchemy: The Secret Art*. London: Thames and Hudson.

de Vries, Ad. *Dictionary of Symbols and Imagery*. 1974. Amsterdam: North-Holland Publishing Co.

Ebin, Victoria. 1979. *The Body Decorated*. London: Thames and Hudson.

Edinger, Edward F. 1985. *Anatomy of the Psyche*. La Salle, IL: Open Court.

——. 1973. *Ego and Archetype*. Baltimore: Penguin Books Inc.

——. 1978. *Melville's Moby-Dick:* A Jungian Commentary. New York: New Directions.

——. 1984. The *Creation of Consciousness*. Toronto: Inner City Books.

——. 1994. *The Eternal Drama*. Boston: Shambhala Publications.

Elder, George F. 1996. *The Body: An Encyclopedia of Archetypal Symbolism*. Boston: Shambhala.

Eliade, Mircea. 1958. *Rites and Symbols of Initiation*. New York: Harper & Row.

Eyo, Ekpo and Willett, Frank. 1982. *Treasures of Ancient Nigeria*. New York: Alfred A. Knopf.

Gimbutas, Marija. 1982. *The Goddesses and Gods of Old Europe*. London: Thames and Hudson.

_____. 1989. *The Language of the Goddess*. San Francisco: Harper & Row.

Hannah, Barbara. 1981. *Encounters with the Soul: Active Imagination as Developed by C.G. Jung*. Santa Monica: Sigo Press.

Hastings, James, ed. 1921. *Encyclopedia of Religion and Ethics*. Edinburgh: T. and T. Clark, 13 vols.

_____. Cowan, H. "Stigmata," vol. 11, pp. 857–860.

_____. Jenkinson, Constance. "Tatuing," vol. 12, pp. 208–214.

_____. Oesterley, W.O.E. "Badges," vol. 2, pp. 325–328.

Jobes, Gertrude. 1962. *Dictionary of Mythology Folklore and Symbols*. New York: The Scarecrow Press, Inc.

Jung, C.G. 1953–1979. *The Collected Works of C.G. Jung*, translated by R.F.C. Hull, edited by H. Read, M. Fordham, G. Adler, Wm. McGuire. Bollingen Series XX (Princeton: Princeton University Press):

_____. *Aion*, vol. 9–2.

_____. *Alchemical Studies*, vol. 13.

_____. *The Archetypes and the Collective Unconscious*, vol. 9–1.

_____. *Mysterium Coniunctionis*, vol. 14.

_____. *Psychology and Alchemy*, vol. 12.

_____. *Psychology and Religion: West and East*, vol. 11.

_____. *Symbols of Transformation*, vol. 5.

_____. *The Development of Personality*, vol. 17.

_____. *The Spirit In Man, Art, And Literature*, vol. 15.

_____. 1984. *Dream Analysis: Notes of the Seminar Given in 1928–1930*. Princeton NJ: Princeton University Press.

_____. 1963. *Memories, Dreams, Reflections*. New York: Pantheon Books/Random House.

_____. 1988. *Nietzsche's Zarathustra: Notes of the Seminar Given in 1934–1939*, ed. James L. Jarrett. Princeton: Princeton University Press.

_____. 1976. *The Visions Seminars*. 2 vols. Zurich: Spring Publications.

_____. and C. Kerényi. 1963. *Essays on a Science of Mythology.* New York: Harper & Row.

Jacobi, Jolande, ed. 1951. *Paracelsus: Selected Writings.* Princeton, NJ: Princeton University Press.

Kan, Michael; Meighan, Clement; and Nicholson, H.B. 1989. *Sculpture of Ancient West Mexico: Nayarit, Jalisco, Colima.* Los Angeles: Los Angeles County Museum of Art and University of New Mexico.

Lifton, Robert Jay. 1967. *Death in Life: Survivors of Hiroshima.* New York: Basic Books, Inc.

Lincoln, Bruce. 1981. *Emerging from the Chrysalis: Studies in Rituals of Women's Initiation.* Cambridge: Harvard University Press.

Meador, Betty De Shong. 2000. *Inanna, Lady of Largest Heart: Poems of the High Priestess Enheduanna.* Austin: University of Texas Press.

Neumann, Erich. 1973. *The Child.* New York: G.P. Putnam's Sons.

Porteus, Stanley D. *The Psychology of a Primitive People: A Study of the Australian Aborigine.* London: Edward Arnold and Co., 1931; reprinted Manchester, NH: Ayer Company Publishers, Inc., 1977.

Roberts, Mary Nooter and Allen F. 1996. *Luba Art and the Making of History.* New York: The Museum for African Art.

Rubin, Arnold (ed.). 1988. *Marks of Civilization.* Los Angeles: Museum of Cultural History.

Shelley, Walter B. 1972. *Consultations in Dermatology with Walter B. Shelley.* 2 vols. Philadelphia: W. B. Saunders Company.

Slattery, Dennis P. 2000. *The Wounded Body: Remembering the Markings of Flesh.* Albany: State University of New York Press.

Smyth, R. Brough. 1878. *The Aborigines of Victoria: With Notes Relating to the Habits of the Natives of Other Parts of Australia and Tasmania.* London: Trubner and Co.

Strommenger, Eva and Hirmer, Max. 1964. *The Art of Mesopotamia .* London: Thames and Hudson.

Thévoz, Michel. 1984. *The Painted Body.* Geneva: Editions d'Art Albert Skira S.A.

Von Franz, Marie-Louise (ed.). 1966. *Aurora Consurgens.* London: Routledge & Kegan Paul.

Ward, Lynd. 1929. *Gods' Man*. New York: Jonathan Cape and Harrison Smith.

Woodman, Marion. 1985. *The Pregnant Virgin: A Process of Psychological Transformation*. Toronto: Inner City Books.


ARTICLES

De Negri, Eve. 1964. Tribal marks: decorative scars and painted patterns. *Nigeria Magazine* 81: 106–116.

Grignon, J.-L.; Schneck, G.; and Gross, D. 1967. La mauvaise cicatrice cutanee: punition ou destin? *Revue de Stomatologie* 68: 622–635.

Maguire, Anne. 1972. The relationship between the unconscious psyche and the organ of the skin. *Harvest* 18:43–54.

Omo-Dare, P. 1973. Yoruban contributions to the literature on keloids. *Journal of the National Medical Association* 65: 367–372, 406.

Rothenberg, Rose-Emily. 1986. Psychic wounds and body scars: an exploration into the psychology of keloid formation. S*pring* 1986: 141–154.

____. 1983. The orphan archetype. *Psychological Perspectives* 14: 181–194.

# INDEX

211

impact of stepmother's insecurities on, 25-26
relationship between sisters of, 26-27, 74-76
*See also* father; stepmother
fantasy reunion with mother, 49, 51
father
common guilt/loss shared with, 69-70
death of, 40-41
identification with *Gods' Man* by, 30-31
personal admission of guilt from, 73-74
relationship with, 27-28, 70-75
sacrificed by, 72
sympathy/kindness of, 34-35
fears
of abandonment, 23, 42, 49, 50-52
of motherhood/child bearing, 55-56, 58
female initiation rites, 127-128*f*, 129*f*
fertility symbol, 120
fire/family dream, 79, 94
fish dreams, 86-87
fish/mother dream, 91-92
flower (keloid) symbolism, 40, 42-43*f*
frog badge incident, 191
frog dream, 53-54
"The Frog Prince," 53

Garden of Eden, 90
Gerland, Georg, 132
God
body marks representing covenant with, 187
cave dream meaning and, 99
conscious connection to, 39
disease as scourge of, 118*f*
father/daughter relationship and, 75
hidden image inside keloids, 184-190
hidden image inside Mary, 198n.36
regeneration of, 178
scarification reminder of power of, 175
son's birth and favorable side of, 91
tempted by Satan to test Job, 117
*Gods' Man*, 30-31*f*, 52, 63, 71, 74
good-mother catalyst/waiter, 103-104
good-mother family representation, 103
good mother image, 76
grape cluster dream, 190
*griot* (African performers), 154, 155
guilt
admission from father of, 73-74
collective level of psyche in, 69-70
orphan archetype profile and, 48-49
regarding mother's death, 25, 48-49, 111, 112
scars as proof of, 66
transforming red color of, 182
guilt complex, 25, 48-49, 66, 68-69, 111, 112, 182
gypsy card vision, 24

Hawthorne, Nathaniel, 62
healing rituals
African scarification practice as, 125, 126*f*,
164-166, 168
body/soul duality during, 168
clay work as, 58
success of meditation, 39
*See also* mother's return

Herodotus, 133
high school years, 34-36
hippopotami visit, 157
Hiroshima bomb victims, 67*f*-68
Hölderlin, Friedrich, 108
housekeepers, 29
husband
desire to have child by, 55
marriage to, 45-46
surgeries surrounding son's birth, 61

indigenous people
attitudes toward deformity by, 169
ritual involvement of body and, 167-168
scars as "marks of God" belief by, 187
*See also* African journey; scarification rites
individuation process
African journey necessary for, 175-177,
184-185
continuing reenactment of creation in, 117
initiated by body symptom, 18
marking the body as expression of, 136-137
tragic guilt as first step in, 68-69
*See also* journey
initiation rite video (African journey), 157
initiation scarification
described, 126-127*f*
entrance into group through, 135
female, 126-128*f*, 129*f*
male, 128-129
process of making keloid scars during,
127-128
inner animal, 100-101*f*, 102
intellectual culture, 97
intestines clay image, 87-88*f*
Inuit tattoo practices, 132
Iphigenia sacrifice myth, 72

Job's test, 117
journey
African trip as part of, 139-177, 184-185
Maier's mystic, 140
role by unconscious during, 193-194
to uncover keloid archetype, 114-138, 192-194
*See also* individuation process
Jung, C.G.
on body and mind connection, 20
on the enemy within, 49
on fire equivalent to suffering, 99
on guilt as first step in individuation, 68-69
initial introduction to, 36
on Maier's mystic journey, 140
on new life origins from the lowest, 191
on new state of being, 102
ossified fish dream described by, 93
remarks on Mass wine/water mixing,
181-182
on roots of the Self, 19
on salvation through danger, 108
on shards mentioned in Kabbalah, 183
on skin as protection, 66
on snake's connection with divine, 90
on threat to hero's birth and life, 112

mother's return
  acceptance message of, 91
  childhood fantasy of, 49, 51, 70
  first dream of, 104-107, 109
  photographs as symbolism of, 109-110f
  second dream of, 111-112
  See also healing rituals
mourning rituals, 125f, 131f
murder dream, 66-67, 69-70, 94
my father in the mirror painting, 71f
my mother in the colon painting, 91, 92f
my mother going off with Death (painting),
    107-108f, 109
my mother going off with Death (poem), 107
my mother and me photographs, 109-110f
The Mythic Image (Campbell), 64

Native American Sun Dance, 130
Native American women
  painting of mother as, 85f
  protection given by, 102, 167
Neumann, Erich, 48, 52
Nietzsche, Friedrich, 90
Nigerian (Ife) terracotta head, 122, 123f
Nigerian legends, 123-124
Nuba people, 126-128, 130
Nursing mother clay figure, 61f

old lady on the hill image, 105-107
opposition. See duality
Orestes myth, 72-73
orphan archetype
  connection between lapis and, 47, 190
  contributions of colitis on understanding
    of, 93-94
  difficulty accepting adult life by, 90
  explored during analysis, 46-52
  fantasy play manifestation of, 27
  full bloom development of, 26
  guilt as primary in profile of, 48-49
  Mesopotamian art association with, 82-83f,
    84, 99, 192
  opposition forces within, 48-49
  search for real identity by, 21
  as subject of first public lecture, 87, 89
  See also keloid archetype
"orphan stone," 47

paintings
  keloid flower, 42-43f
  of my mother, 85f
  my father in the mirror, 71f
  my mother in the colon, 91, 92f
  my mother going off with Death, 107-108f,
    109
  relationship between scars and, 169-170
  revealing light within darkness, 44f
  during ulcerative colitis illness, 85f-86
  water emerging out of red scar, 55f
  See also artwork
Paleolithic goddess statues, 121f
Paracelsus, 21
pellets of clay on Mexican tomb sculptures, 122f

physical symptoms. See body symptoms
Pietá painting, 97
Plato, 137
Pontius, 133
prayer, 39
priestess dream, 179
prima materia (first matter), 14, 55, 190
projection, 195n.2
psyche
  archetypal image emerging from hole in,
    200n.62
  body symptom manifested from, 18-19,
    175
  giving birth to unborn parts of, 13
  guilt and collective level of, 69-70
  keloid flower meaning to, 40
  living in shadow of father's, 70
  mother painting revelations of, 85f-86
  physical manifestation of, 20
  preparing for reunion with mother, 104
  presence of rage in, 87
  returning to principle of opposites in, 119
  role of scars in duality of, 63, 135
  scarification as protecting the, 134-135
  scars as expression of conflict within, 46
  the Self as center of, 19
  tiger connection to independence of, 77
  See also consciousness
"The Psychological Processes of Speech
    Therapists" (college course), 38

religious clay figures, 56f, 57-58
"The Republic" (Plato), 137
"rites of passage" significance, 96
Roberts, Allen, 133
Roman Empire tattoo/scarification practices,
    132

sacrifice
  association of Christ, lion and, 97
  Bagassi chicken, 148f-151f
  broken plate dream about, 182-183
  to father, 72
  mother's death reconceptualized as,
    111-112
  return to inner village through, 170-171
sandtray therapy tool, 49-50
scarification rites
  for cultivating piety, 133
  "The Elixir of Life" and, 134
  going to Africa to research, 139-160
  historical practices of, 132-133
  initiation, 126-129
  mourning, 125f, 131f
  as protection, 134-135
  relationship between death and, 163
  as reminder of God's power, 175
  shaman interviews regarding, 161f-173f
scars. See keloid scars
the Self
  clay work support through, 58
  conscious realization of, 181
  fire symbolism of endurance of, 101

215